ALONG LOST LINES

PAUL ATTERBURY

A DAVID & CHARLES BOOK

Copyright © David & Charles Limited 2007

David & Charles is an F+W Publications Inc. company
4700 East Galbraith Road
Cincinnati, OH 45236

First published in the UK in 2007

Copyright © Paul Atterbury 2007

Paul Atterbury has asserted his right to be identified as author of this work
in accordance with the Copyright, Designs and Patents Act, 1988.

A catalogue record for this book is available from the British Library.

ISBN-13 978-0-7153-2568-1
ISBN-10: 0-7153-2568-X

Printed in Singapore by KHL Printing Co Pte Ltd
Brunel House, Newton Abbot, Devon

Produced for David & Charles by
OutHouse Publishing
Shalbourne, Marlborough, Wiltshire SN8 3QJ

For OutHouse Publishing
Project Manager & Editor: Sue Gordon
Designer & Picture Researcher: Julian Holland
Design Assistants: Nigel White, Dawn Terrey

For David & Charles
Commissioning Editor: Mic Cady
Head of Design: Prudence Rogers
Assistant Editor: Louise Clark
Production Controller: Beverley Richardson

Visit our website at www.davidandcharles.co.uk

David & Charles books are available from all good bookshops; alternatively you
can contact our Orderline on 0870 9908222 or write to us at FREEPOST EX2
110, D&C Direct, Newton Abbot, TQ12 4ZZ (no stamp required UK only);
US customers call 800-289-0963 and Canadian customers call 800-840-5220.

▼ A classic example of the lost railway in the landscape is to be
seen near Colfin, on the old line from Stranraer south to Portpatrick,
where the grassy embankment cuts through the rounded hills.

ALONG LOST LINES

Discovering the glorious heritage of yesterday's railways

PAUL ATTERBURY

D&C
David and Charles

CONTENTS

INTRODUCTION

▲ The railways were littered with enamel and cast-iron signs identifying places or giving warnings or instructions. This one, associated with a signal box, is entertainingly obscure.

The railway map of Britain is covered with lost journeys. Since the 1960s thousands of miles of track and thousands of stations have been closed. Over the last fifty years railways have become rather different, with politics, economics and changing social habits all playing a part, and the extent of that loss, and the changes it provoked, is now being appreciated and reassessed. Romance and nostalgia are vital components in railway history, and the railway experience, today. This indicates that the losses go beyond the track, the stations and the trains, for what disappeared in that period of change was a way of life that was at the very heart of British culture. This book takes a broad view of what the closure programme meant, at the time and subsequently, and looks at many aspects of railway life, once taken for granted and now often forgotten, that vanished along with the track and the trains. Nowadays railway history is more popular than ever, and bound up with that history is a wealth of personal memories, which this book aims to release.

▲ Exploring lost railways is a national pastime. Hundreds of miles of old railways have been turned into official footpaths and cycleways, while hundreds more remain lost, often on private land and inaccessible without permission. The pleasures of the overgrown track and a points lever that could still be operated at the former military sidings near Warcop, in Yorkshire, is not lost on this child on a visit in the 1990s.

▲ Informal photographs are a wonderful record of lost railways. Particularly appealing are groups of station staff, such as this 1920s example. The men are arranged casually, around the porter's cart, yet show real pride in the job. The station dog, seated on the milk churn, is clearly in charge.

▶ Railway postcards have been produced in an astonishing variety since the early 1900s, many by the railway companies themselves for promotional purposes. Others, issued by postcard publishers, show trains, stations and other aspects of railway life. They are a real insight into the way railways used to be. This classic scene shows the North Eastern Railway's Leeds-to-Glasgow breakfast and luncheon car express.

▼ The appeal of the railways at their peak lay in their diversity. The network on the Isle of Wight was notably distinctive, independent and memorable for its eccentricity. This little signal cabin, with its delightful notice, was at Bembridge until the 1960s.

RAILWAY · EXECUTIVE
SHOOTING, FISHING AND
EGGING PROHIBITED.
BY ORDER.

THE BEECHING REPORT

The publication in 1963 of the infamous report entitled *The Reshaping of British Railways* brought into public prominence the name of Dr Richard Beeching, who had become chairman of the British Transport Commission in 1961. Given the task of reversing the steady decline of railways in Britain, he approached the problem in a dispassionate, direct and cost-based manner. His proposal – the closure of more than 2,000 stations and thousands of miles of railway and the withdrawal of over 250 train services – caused a furore throughout the country. There were many bitter battles, but few lines scheduled for closure escaped his axe and Beeching's name became synonymous with the destruction of Britain's railways. This was in some ways unjust, for much of what Beeching recommended was inevitable. More importantly, the second part of his report, *The Development of Major Trunk Routes*, was ignored by government. Had his advice been followed, Britain could have had a modern network that the world would have envied.

Map No. 9

BRITISH RAILWAYS PROPOSED WITHDRAWAL OF PASSENGER TRAIN SERVICES

All passenger services to be withdrawn ————

All stopping passenger services to be withdrawn =========

Services, which were under consideration in August 1962, and which, in some cases, have already been withdrawn, are included in this map.

BRITISH RAILWAYS BOARD

The Reshaping of British Railways

PART 1: REPORT

LONDON
HER MAJESTY'S STATIONERY OFFICE

◀ Public Notices announcing the proposed closure of lines and stations became commonplace through the 1960s and into the 1970s. This one, dated 1971, proposed a closure that did not take place; the line is still open.

▲ Dr Beeching's highly detailed report makes interesting reading. It addressed both freight and passenger traffic. Twelve maps supported the lists of services to be withdrawn and stations to be closed (some of which are named across these pages).

An objection has been received and the withdrawal of this
BRITISH RAILWAYS BOARD
by the Transport Users' Consultative Committee

PUBLIC NOTICE
TRANSPORT ACT - 1962

Withdrawal of Railway Passenger Services

The Secretary of State for the Environment has said that he is unlikely to renew the grant for the Machynlleth to Pwllheli passenger train service after the end of 1971, unless he has previously refused consent to a statutory closure proposal.

Accordingly the London Midland Region of British Railways hereby give notice in accordance with Section 56(7) of the Transport Act 1962, that they propose to discontinue all railway passenger services between :—

MACHYNLLETH and PWLLHELI

involving the discontinuance of all passenger services from the following section of line :—

DOVEY JUNCTION — PWLLHELI

and from the following stations :—

ABERDOVEY	HARLECH	PENRHYNDEUDRAETH
ABERERCH	LLANABER	PENYCHAIN
ABERTAFOL	LLANBEDR & PENSARN	PORTMADOC
BARMOUTH	LLANDANWG	PWLLHELI
BLACK ROCK	LLANDECWYN	TALSARNAU
CRICCIETH	LLANGELYNIN	TALWRN BACH
DOVEY JUNCTION	LLWYNGWRIL	TALYBONT
DYFFRYN ARDUDWY	MINFFORDD	TONFANAU
FAIRBOURNE	MORFA MAWDDACH	TOWYN
GOGARTH	PENHELIG	TYGWYN

It appears to the Board that the following alternative services will be available :—

EXISTING SERVICES BY RAIL — NONE AVAILABLE

EXISTING SERVICES BY ROAD — Crosville Motor Services Ltd.,
Service No. 82a/27 PWLLHELI & MAENTWROG
Service No. S35 MAENTWROG & BARMOUTH
Service No. S34 BARMOUTH & DOLGELLAU
Service No. S28 DOLGELLAU & TOWYN
Service No. S26 TOWYN & MACHYNLLETH

Any users of the rail service which it is proposed to discontinue and anybody representing such users may lodge an objection in writing within six weeks of 27th MARCH 1971, i.e. not later than 8th MAY 1971, addressing the objection to :—

The Secretary, Transport Users' Consultative Committee
for the Wales and Monmouthshire Area,
22 The Chambers,
68 St. Mary's Street,
Cardiff. CF1 1FD.

If any objection is lodged the service cannot be discontinued until the Transport Users' Consultative Committee has considered the objections and reported to the Secretary of State for the Environment and the Secretary has given consent to the Closure under Section 56(8) of the Transport Act 1962.

The Committee may hold a meeting to hear objections. Such a meeting will be held in public and any persons who have lodged an objection in writing may also make oral representations to the Committee.

If no objections are lodged to the proposal the service will be discontinued and the stations closed on **4th October 1971.**

▶ Prior to Beeching, line closures had attracted little attention, but afterwards every one aroused great interest, and images of last trains became all too familiar. This one is at Ryde Esplanade, on the Isle of Wight, on New Year's Eve, 1966.

HARESFIELD HARTLEY HATHERLEIGH HATHERSAGE HAVENHOUS
DON HEELEY HELE AND BRADNINCH HELMSHOR
SEA OAKAMOOR OAK
MESBY OR
CHERS HAM THAN
IBARDINE TYNEHE
HALT W INCH
WEDNESBURY TOWN
WHOUSES
HERSAGE HILL
NBURY ISAL
OAKLE
OSS ITLEY OTI MAR
THANK ON THOMS HALT
RDINE TYNEH UDNY JE DWEL
WHITEINCH ERSIDE YOKER FERRY W OUGH
WANSTEAD K WARNG TCHE
WEDNESBURY TOWN WELFORD NGTO
BLACKWELL AIGH HALTON
HOUSE HAV L HAWS

BEECHINGS CLOSE

▲ A curious byproduct of the Beeching era is that his name is commemorated on minor roads all over Britain, usually on housing estates built on the sites of former stations. This recent example is on the site of Wisbech St Mary station.

▼ A familiar sight all over Britain in the 1960s was the work of the demolition gangs, removing track and infrastructure following closure. This is near Notgrove, Gloucestershire, in May 1964.

MERRYMAKER
Last Ride
on the
Wallingford Branch
Sunday 31 May 1981
£5·50 2nd class   £8 1st class

We are going to have a jolly 'wake' on Sunday 31 May to mark the closure of the Wallingford branch line. A special train will leave London Paddington at approx. 10 00 hours and run via Aylesbury, Claydon Jcn., Bicester, Oxford (break for refreshments) then for a final ride on the branch line, before returning through Reading to Paddington.

Accommodation limited, make sure of a place for the 'Wallingford Wake' by applying early for your tickets to:

Chief Booking Clerk
No.1 Platform, British Rail Western
Paddington, LONDON W7.

This is the age of the train ⇌

▲ Most closures had happened by the early 1970s, but the Beeching legacy lingered on. One of the last, at this stage seen by British Rail as something to celebrate, was the Wallingford branch, in 1981.

THE WEST
COUNTRY

LOST & FOUND

A REMOTE PATH with wonderful views, high above the rocky shore, was once the trackbed of the old branch to Easton, on Portland, Dorset.

◄ WATERGATE HALT, on the rural Devon line from Bideford to Halwill, was never much of a place, yet its simple platform survives, overgrown but largely unchanged since the trains stopped in 1965.

▼ ONE OF ENGLAND'S BEST examples of spectacular railway landscape is the route of the former Princetown branch across Dartmoor. Much of it can be walked.

▼ When lines close, metal bridges are usually taken away because of their scrap value and because they obstruct the roads. Survivors are quite rare. This one crosses a very minor road near Powerstock, on the former Bridport branch in Dorset.

▲ The Somerset & Dorset was a once mighty railway, much lamented when it closed. Plenty survives, waiting to be discovered. At Horsington a powerful bridge crosses the track.

GWINEAR ROAD TO HELSTON

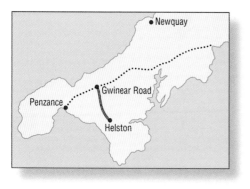

ornish branch lines tend to have long histories, linked as they were to the development of industries, mines and harbours. The Helston branch tells a different story. Tourism and local business interests were its inspiration, and local promoters ensured that the Helston Railway came into being in July 1880. However, the building of the nearly 9-mile line took longer and cost more than anticipated and it did not open until 1887. Later there was a plan to extend the line beyond Helston to the Lizard but costs made this impractical. Instead the railway pioneered the use of connecting buses for the journey to the Lizard. It was here that the first Great Western Railway buses appeared, on 1 August 1903, the GWR having purchased the line five years earlier. The line was single-track throughout and the terminus at Helston was limited by there being only one platform. In its early years the line was kept busy by expanding tourist traffic and there was regular freight traffic, including those Cornish staples, cauliflower and broccoli.

The line branched away from the main line at Gwinear Road, to the west of Camborne, a remote junction far from any town or village. Gwinear village

◄ Sometimes when railways disappear they leave surprising things behind. It is more than forty years since closure, yet the signpost in Carnhell Green still points to Gwinear Road station.

▼ It is August 1962 and in three months the line will be closed. Yet Helston is still busy. Locomotive D6353 has just brought in the 10.55 from Gwinear Road, boxes and packets are piled up on the platform and, to the left, ladies in summer dresses are waiting for the bus to the Lizard.

▲ On a line of minor stations, Truthall Halt was one of the smallest. Yet beneath the old stone road bridge traces of the platform remain, half buried with earth and overgrown. There is currently a plan to reopen this section of the route.

was over a mile away and, despite the station name, there was no direct road to it. Yet a sizeable railway community grew up around the junction and its station, which had extensive sidings. There were five stations between Gwinear Road and Helston, two of which were unadvertised ticket platforms, where trains stopped by request. The route, remote and meandering, was through a dramatic landscape, with typically Cornish views. Decline set in during the 1950s, yet in 1961 there were still ten trains on weekdays. By then the branch was a clear candidate for closure, and the end for passengers came in November 1962. Freight continued for another couple of years and then in 1965 Gwinear Road station was closed as well.

Today plenty survives to be seen, although much of the trackbed is private and inaccessible. Little remains of Gwinear Road or the junction but traces can be found of other stations. At Nancegollan a station lamp can be seen, rising above the densely overgrown platform. There are cuttings and embankments but the main engineering feature was the big stone viaduct over the river Cober, which to this day looks splendid in the woods when seen from the distant B3302. It can also be seen close to from minor roads. Nothing remains of Helston station.

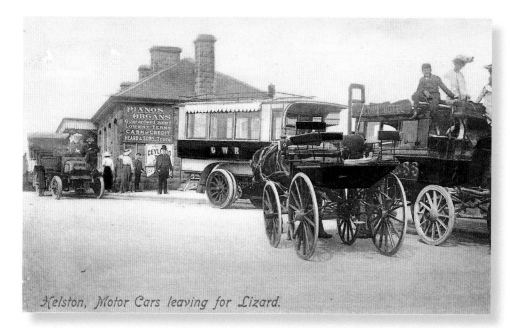

Helston, Motor Cars leaving for Lizard.

▲ The GWR ran its first buses from Helston station to the Lizard. The service started in 1903 and this card is only a few years later.

▼ On a sunny day in the 1950s at Helston station everyone – the station staff, the lady in a white shirt and the two small boys – is waiting for something to happen. The goods shed and sidings are busy.

▼ The major engineering feature on the Helston branch was the stone viaduct over the river Cober and this still stands. Here is what would have been the engine-driver's view of this imposing stone structure, with its curving trackbed now choked with gorse.

EVERCREECH JUNCTION TO BURNHAM-ON-SEA

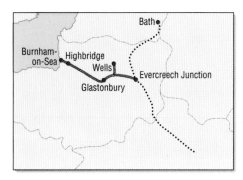

Somerset was well served by railways in the 19th century, particularly in the largely rural triangle formed by Bristol, Taunton and Yeovil. Some of these, like the canals that preceded them, were inspired by the Somerset coal fields but, that apart, there was little industry in the region. Coastal harbours and ports and river estuaries were still busy, and they fuelled the hopes of railway promoters. In the 1850s several railway companies were authorized, including the East Somerset, the West Somerset and the Somerset Central. Another scheme under way in this region was the Dorset Central, whose line from Wimborne to Cole was completed early in 1862. By this time, the Somerset Central had opened its line from Highbridge to Glastonbury, with branches to Burnham pier and Wells, plus a later extension eastwards towards Cole. This was originally a broad-gauge line, supported by the Bristol & Exeter, and thus the GWR. In the early 1860s it was converted to standard gauge and merged with the Dorset Central to form the famous Somerset & Dorset Railway in 1862. Ambitious plans to extend north to Bath from Evercreech were undermined by financial problems and, though completed in 1874, bankruptcy

▼ Today there is little to indicate that Evercreech was ever a busy railway junction, yet it was here that in 1874 the new Somerset & Dorset main line to Bath met the existing Highbridge line. Sheep now graze in the empty fields where mighty locomotives used to meet. Here, in October 1965, a Bournemouth-to-Bristol express pauses at Evercreech Junction beside the local for Highbridge.

▼ Much of the route westwards from Evercreech can be identified, though access is not always possible. Here, near West Pennard, the line of the trackbed can still be seen, now used as a farm access track.

▲ Glastonbury and Street was a substantial station, for it was here that the Wells branch met the Highbridge line. On this occasion, probably in the 1920s, things were quiet and the photographer could take his time.

▼ Always independently minded, the S&D has long been the favourite of many enthusiasts. Surviving paperwork, such as this 1900s carriage note from Bournemouth goods department, is much sought after.

soon followed and the network was leased by the Midland and the London & South Western, who formed the Somerset & Dorset Joint Railway. While the Bath-to-Bournemouth route became the main line, Highbridge remained important, not least because the company's works was located there. A century after they were built, in the 1960s, most of Somerset's railways were swept away, including the Somerset & Dorset. The main line and the branch from Evercreech to Highbridge closed in 1966.

From Evercreech to Glastonbury there is not much to be seen today and the surviving trackbed and stations, at Pylle and West Pennard, are on private land. West of Glastonbury the route is a cycleway and footpath (Sustrans Route 3) as far as Shapwick. Old bridges include one over the river Brue. At Edington Route 3 turns away to follow the Bridgwater branch. Nothing remains at Highbridge or Burnham.

▲ Sometimes unexpected survivals, such as this level-crossing gatepost west of Glastonbury, are the only things to indicate that there was once a railway there.

◄ Edington Burtle, seen here in October 1965, was a typical S&D country station, marking the junction with the line south to Bridgwater.

► Standing on the footbridge, this photographer appears to have taken great care with the arrangement of his picture of Highbridge level crossing, posing the signalman and the pedestrians and catching the horse and cart at the right moment. Signals show that no trains were due.

▼ When railways are closed, the track and much of the infrastructure, particularly the metalwork, soon disappears. This metal bridge west of Glastonbury survives, now used for farm access.

LOST STATIONS: THE WEST COUNTRY

Prior to the coming of the railways, Cornwall, Devon and much of Somerset were relatively inaccessible and it was both difficult and expensive to travel around this part of England. Major centres such as Exeter, Plymouth and Taunton were connected to the network quite early but the rest of the region had to wait until the latter part of the Victorian period. The main line to Penzance was completed by 1860, but other main lines, for example the LSWR route westwards from Exeter to North Cornwall and the Somerset & Dorset's line south from Bath to Bournemouth, came much later. The West Country was also the home of the branch line, particularly in Devon and Cornwall, with many rural communities and local industries depending on them. Local railways of this kind were one of the prime targets for closure in the 1960s, and many rural routes and branch lines disappeared, plunging country areas and small towns and villages back into relative isolation. Devon and Cornwall were hard hit, but so was Somerset, particularly north of Yeovil and Taunton, and around Wells and Shepton Mallet, where trains vanished completely. Main lines were also affected, notably the Somerset & Dorset and most of its connecting network, and the meandering tentacles of the north Cornwall railway, the latter serviced so effectively for years by the many sections of the famous Atlantic Coast Express. All this and much more went, as well as countless stations great and small, along with their associated buildings.

▲ In 1969 a class 35 diesel runs light through the remains of Mangotsfield station, by then reduced to a curtain wall. Formerly an important junction on the Midland line into Bath and Bristol, it closed progressively from 1966. Today, the trackbed is part of a cycleway.

▼ Perranporth, on the north Cornwall line between Newquay and Chacewater, was a near-perfect station: a lovely setting, a pretty building with echoes of Brunel, a goods shed and yard, water columns and a signal box. Luckily for the lorry parked on the track on this day in 1959, it was also quiet. The line closed in 1963.

▲ These are the ruins of Luxborough Road, an untimetabled station on a branch of the West Somerset Mineral Railway. Built to serve mines in the Brendon Hills, the line opened in 1859, complete with inclined plane and, from 1865, six stations. Passenger services ceased in 1898.

▼ Tavistock had two stations, one served by the LSWR, the other by the GWR. Both went to Plymouth. This is the Great Western's covered South station. A train is leaving on the branch to Launceston. The line closed in 1962.

▲ Whitehall Halt, on the Devon branch line to Hemyock from Tiverton, was the most minimal station imaginable. It closed in 1963 but bizarrely it survives, virtually intact, in a private garden.

LOST JOURNEY: BUDLEIGH SALTERTON

Until the 1960s there were a number of railway routes that crossed Devon and Cornwall from one coast to the other, but today the branch from Par to Newquay, in Cornwall, is the only line that traverses the peninsula. Prior to the 1960s there were several options for people travelling between the north coast and the south, a journey that would have been made by friends visiting each other, families on holiday and people travelling for work, particularly when the train represented the only practical method of transport. Complicated journeys involving a number of changes were a matter of course, and station staff were well used to planning them. A typical crossing of the West Country was from Bude to Budleigh Salterton, from one resort on the north coast of Cornwall to another on the more sheltered coast of east Devon. In the 1930s and 1940s this involved three changes with good connections and took a little over 4 hours. Today that journey is impossible, though sections of the route, from Exmouth to Exeter and from Exeter to Crediton and, occasionally, Okehampton, survive.

TIMETABLE	
Bude............................	8.00am
Okehampton......................	9.17am
Change	
Okehampton......................	9.33am
Exeter Central..................	10.23am
Change	
Exeter Central	10.45am
Exmouth.........................	11.12am
Change	
Exmouth.........................	12.10pm
Budleigh Salterton.............	12.21pm

BUDE — Holsworthy — Halwill Junction — OKEHAMPTON

◀ BUDE, A RESORT FAMOUS for its magnificent beaches, acquired its railway quite late, in 1898. A small terminus station was at the end of a long branch from Okehampton via Halwill Junction, one of a number of lines driven westwards from the 1870s to the 1890s by the London & South Western Railway in order to attack the Great Western's dominance of West Country freight and holiday traffic. At its peak, Bude was served by the famous Atlantic Coast Express from Waterloo. Here, shortly before closure in 1966, a local DMU is ready to depart.

▶ OKEHAMPTON WAS A BUSY station on the London & South Western's main line from Exeter to Plymouth. When the tentacles of the North Cornwall lines spread westwards, Okehampton became important as an interchange station for passengers and, equally, freight, as can be seen here. The station is set high above the town, so, with only about 15 minutes between trains on this journey, there was no time to explore. Closed to passengers in the 1960s, the line was kept open for stone traffic from nearby Meldon quarry. It now has occasional passenger use.

◄ EXETER CENTRAL, formerly Queen Street, is well placed in the city centre, and convenient for shops, the Royal Albert Museum and the cathedral. It opened in 1860 and was rebuilt by the Southern Railway in 1933 with an elegant Queen Anne style frontage. On this journey, with about 20 minutes between trains, there would only have been time for a quick walk, or perhaps a cup of coffee. However, there would have been time to send this postcard, with views of some of the city's highlights. The station is still used today.

Crediton

EXETER

► THE LINE FROM EXETER TO EXMOUTH was completed in 1861 and is still open. For much of the way it runs along the eastern shore of the Exe estuary, and from Topsham on there are fine views across the water. This card depicts the view of the estuary, as seen from the carriage window. With an hour to wait between trains, there is time to explore.

EXMOUTH

BUDLEIGH SALTERTON

◄ BUDLEIGH SALTERTON, a quiet Devon resort, acquired its station in 1897, the terminus of a branch from the Sidmouth line. In 1903 this was extended westwards to Exmouth, a 10-minute ride to bring this journey to its end.

THE PULLMAN TRAIN

George Pullman developed the idea of the luxury railway carriage that bears his name in America and then brought it to Britain in the 1870s. Pullmans were owned, managed, maintained and staffed independently and were operated in conjunction with railway companies, who either added them to existing services or ran dedicated Pullman trains. Passengers paid a supplement, and service was superior to conventional first class, with food and drink served at-seat. Pullman's first British contract was with the Midland Railway in 1873 and other companies soon followed. Pullman died in 1897, by which time the Pullman carriage and train were well established, being operated by the Pullman Palace Car Company (from 1915 the Pullman Car Co.).

From the start, Pullmans were distinctive vehicles with flat body sides and vestibules at each end. There were several types, including parlour, restaurant and bar cars. The famous brown-and-cream livery with its ornate lining was

▼ The most famous Pullman train, the Brighton Belle, ran from 1933 to 1972. Here, in its last year, it crosses Balcombe viaduct near Haywards Heath, Sussex, on its way to London Victoria.

▶ 'The Age of the Train' was a 1980s British Rail marketing slogan, applied here to the last Pullman generation

THE MANCHESTER
PULLMAN

Pullma

This is the age of th

established by 1906 and each carriage had a name or number emblazoned on the sides. From the 1920s British Pullman trains began to acquire names, usually based on the destination, such as the Brighton Belle or the West Riding Pullman, and this practice was maintained until the end of British Railways in the 1990s. Another popular use was as boat trains. In the meantime, in 1962, Pullman had become a part of British Railways. Until this date, Pullmans built in various railway workshops in Britain were all constructed and finished to the same standard, although there were minor variations in decoration. For example, some had marquetry panels, while others used lacquer, and styles ranged from 18th-century Revival to Art Deco.

From 1960 British Railways introduced an entirely new type of luxury train, the Blue Pullman, based on modern-looking, self-contained diesel electric train sets. Until 1973 these operated between London and Manchester, Bristol, Birmingham and Swansea. In the 1980s the final generation of Pullmans appeared, operated by British Rail's Intercity division. However, these were conventional first-class vehicles, with only the at-seat service being retained from the traditional Pullman concept, and were aimed largely at the business user. These came to an end with the destruction of British Rail in the privatization of the 1990s. Some classic Pullmans survive on special trains such as the Venice Simplon-Orient-Express.

In their heyday, classic Pullmans were often used for special trains carrying royalty or visiting heads of state, or for great state occasions such as the funeral of Sir Winston Churchill in 1965.

▲ Until the 1920s, the Pullman name was not always used to describe luxury express trains and there were many variations in the livery. This card shows the Hastings Car Train of about 1905, operated by the South Eastern & Chatham Railway.

▼ In 1968 the Blue Pullman from London Paddington approaches Bristol, its destination. The road it crosses is choked with traffic: even then, it was quicker by train.

▼ The West Riding was a famous Pullman service, probably at its peak in the 1930s. Here, at some point in that decade, the down West Riding passes through Harringay, on the outskirts of London, hauled by A3 Pacific no. 2747.

▲ The Southern Belle, operated by the London, Brighton & South Coast Railway, was the precursor of the Brighton Belle. By 1910, the date of this card, the familiar brown-and-cream Pullman livery was established, to remain unchanged until the 1960s.

Tees-Tyne Pullman

The premier InterCity First Class service for the business traveller.
Travel by Pullman at no extra cost, from Newcastle, Durham, Darlington or York to London.

13 January – 9 May 1986

We're getting there ≷ InterCity

▶ This 1986 leaflet promotes the Tees-Tyne Pullman, one of the last generation of Pullman services operated by British Rail.

A LOST ROYAL TRAIN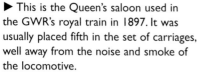

The first royal carriage was built by the Great Western Railway in 1840, and other companies, notably the London & Birmingham and the South Eastern, which served routes used frequently by the Queen and the royal family, soon added royal vehicles to their fleets. These early, and rather uncomfortable, four-wheelers were soon replaced by large, more luxurious carriages, culminating in a twelve-wheeler put into service by the LNWR in 1895. By this time royal trains (and there were always several of them) were composed of dedicated sets of specially built vehicles catering for all the needs of the Queen, her family and the staff. The arrangements for any royal journey were complex in the extreme, and frequently caused considerable disruption to timetabled services along the route. Queen Victoria travelled extensively around Britain during the celebration of her golden and diamond jubilees, in 1887 and 1897, and companies who carried her regularly, such as the Great Western, either built new royal trains or refurbished existing ones. These pictures show the train used by the GWR in 1897.

▲ Queen Victoria, seen here in 1887, enjoyed train travel but insisted that speeds be kept to a maximum of 40mph. The jubilee celebrations caused her popularity to soar, and she travelled extensively around her kingdom.

▶ This is the Queen's saloon used in the GWR's royal train in 1897. It was usually placed fifth in the set of carriages, well away from the noise and smoke of the locomotive.

▼ The 1897 GWR royal train had a dedicated locomotive, suitably named 'The Queen'. Built in Swindon in 1894, no. 3041 was originally called 'Emlyn'.

▲ The interior of the royal saloon was sumptuous but discreet and finished to the highest standard. There was electric light, and a bell to summon the guard. This is the view into the Queen's compartment from the area used by the maids of honour.

▲ Looking like the most luxurious first-class carriage, complete with framed prints on the partition walls, this is actually the smoking saloon, with gentleman's lavatory.

▲ This view shows the rather more spartan interior of the guard's van, with kitchen and water heating equipment, and the handbrake in the foreground.

TAKING THE TRAIN

Trains, and particularly their locomotives, have always had an appeal to the enthusiast. However, it is the wider relationship between trains and people that is so much more interesting. Trains are about journeys, and for most people it is the journey, rather than the train, that sticks in the mind. Modern trains are efficient, quick and relatively comfortable, even if often overcrowded, but they also lack character. As these photographs show, a train journey used to be something to celebrate, for the railway was, until the 1970s, at the centre of life. Much has been lost in the process of surrender to the motor car, and not simply the splendours of steam and the universality of train travel. Regional variations and local detail have disappeared. Windows can rarely be opened and doors are automatic. Concerns about security and safety have limited access to platforms, thereby reducing the sense of excitement that always accompanied departure and arrival. Passengers have become customers and journeys are terminated.

▲ A contented girl relaxes in the spacious and elegant air-conditioned comfort of a Bristol-bound Intercity express in 1973 as she lets the train take the strain.

◄ On 14 August, a Wednesday morning, in 1929, a smart woman poses at an unidentified station. Has she just arrived, or is she leaving? Either way, she is feeling cheerful about the journey.

► Four scouts, crowded into the open window, share the excitement of departure as they set off from Brighton for a jamboree.

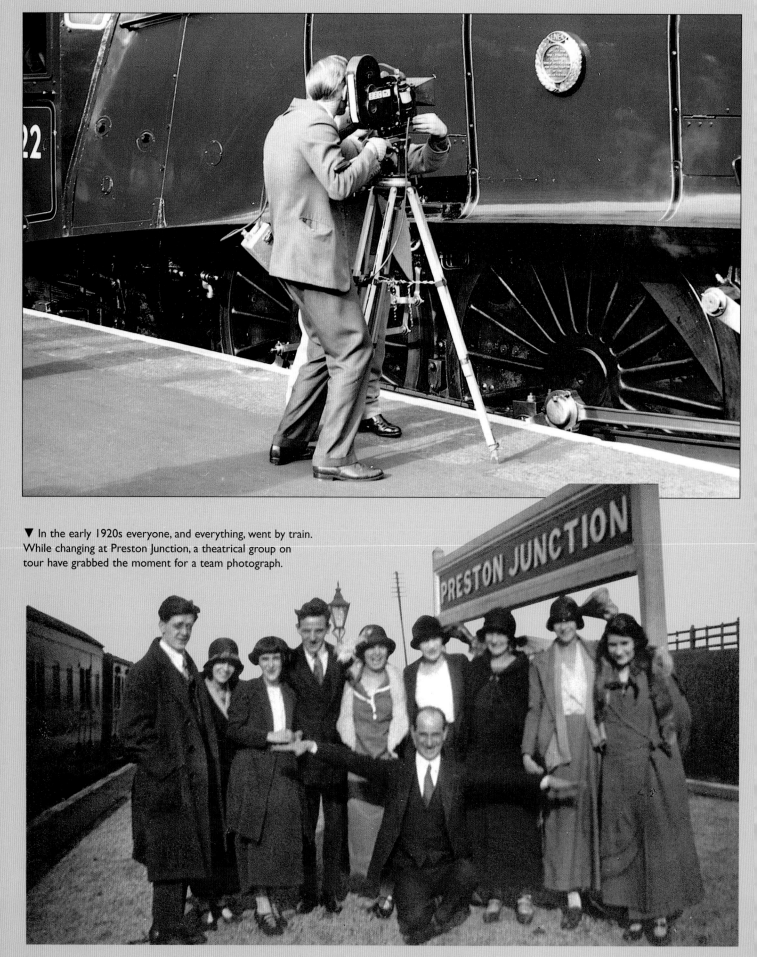

▼ In the early 1920s everyone, and everything, went by train. While changing at Preston Junction, a theatrical group on tour have grabbed the moment for a team photograph.

PRESTON JUNCTION

◄ A professional enthusiast, his passion clearly apparent, crouches behind his BBC TV camera to film the plaque on the famous A4 Pacific 'Mallard' that commemorates her world-record breaking high-speed run.

► It is a grey day at Paddington as 4079 'Pendennis Castle' prepares to haul a west-bound express out of the station. A jolly chap, well dressed apart from his rather short trousers, poses for the camera. The caption, 'R.B. after lunch!' says it all.

▼ Young boys of all ages await the departure of 34082 '615 Squadron' from the very end of a Waterloo platform – an unlikely scene today.

BOAT TRAINS

The idea of running special trains to carry passengers to and from ships and ferries dates back to the 1840s. Initially they served ports on the Thames and the west coast of Scotland. The first boat train to operate to a regular schedule was the Irish Mail, between London and Holyhead. By the 1880s boat trains were running to ports and harbours all over Britain, serving ferries and, increasingly, ocean liners. At the same time, the quality of service improved, with many companies using dedicated sets of carriages with Pullman-style luxury, equipped to provide catering to a high standard; some, such as the Hook Continental from Liverpool Street to Harwich, were famous for their food. During the 1920s and 1930s many boat trains acquired names, most famously The Golden Arrow, and some of these lived on into the British Railways era. However, they began to disappear from the timetable in the 1960s, and it was not long before all the dedicated and special boat trains had gone. Those that survived into the 1980s, for example to maritime stations at Dover, Newhaven, Weymouth, Harwich or Holyhead, used standard carriages and were boat trains only in name.

BR. 21778/16

BRITISH RAILWAYS

THIS TRAIN RUNS ALONG THE PUBLIC ROADWAY BETWEEN THE QUAY AND THE JUNCTION WITH THE MAIN LINE AT WEYMOUTH. PASSENGERS ARE ASKED NOT TO USE THE LAVATORIES DURING THIS PART OF THE JOURNEY.

▲ While trainspotters and a porter look the other way, a boat train for Tilbury prepares to depart from St Pancras in the summer of 1953.

▼ ▲ The Channel Islands Boat Train makes its way through the streets of Weymouth along the famous quay tramway in the 1970s, its class 33 locomotive armed with bell and flashing light. Services along the tramway continued into the late 1980s.

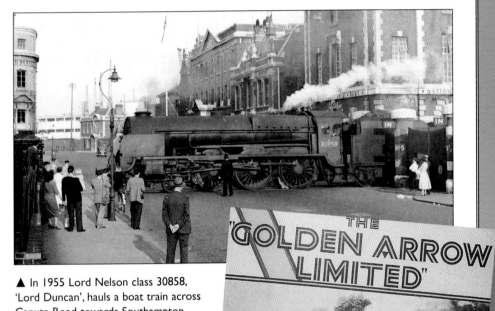

▲ In 1955 Lord Nelson class 30858, 'Lord Duncan', hauls a boat train across Canute Road towards Southampton docks while spectators look on and a policeman makes sure the locomotive behaves.

▼ This Edwardian card shows the South Eastern & Chatham's Folkestone Express.

THE "GOLDEN ARROW LIMITED"

WORLD FAMOUS DE LUXE PULLMAN SERVICE DAILY BETWEEN LONDON [VICTORIA] AND PARIS [NORD]

Copies of the illustration above, in colour, price 1/- and Jig Saw puzzles 5/- each post free from S.R. Advertising Depᵗˢ Waterloo Station, London, S.E.1. and through Messʳˢ W.H.Smith's bookstalls & shops.

PARIS 6½ HOURS

SOUTHERN RAILWAY
KEY TO THE CONTINENT

▲ A famous poster for a famous train: the Southern Railway promotes its premier Pullman boat train service in the 1930s. Only the Channel Tunnel could improve on that journey time.

► A scene at Dover's Marine station in the 1960s as Merchant Navy class no. 35026, 'Lamport & Holt Line', sits at the head of a boat train. This great harbour station is now a car park for the cruise terminal.

SIGNALLING

One of the most familiar features of the railway landscape was the semaphore signal. Standing alone or in small groups, or arranged en masse on a massive gantry across the track, signals were the visible sign of order and control. Signalling started with men waving flags or lamps but a more permanent system soon became necessary. Through the Victorian period, signalling gradually improved, with the drive towards greater clarity, efficiency and standardization usually inspired by accidents. By the end of the 19th century the two types of semaphore signal, red-and-white for home and yellow-and-black with a fishtail end for distant, were widely established, along with their accompanying lights. From the 1860s signals were increasingly controlled from signal boxes and were interlocked with points. The authority and control of the signalman was established formally in 1889 when block working and interlocking were made compulsory. Colour light signalling was first used in the 1920s, then spread rapidly over the network. However, the semaphore signal was still in widespread use in the 1980s, and even today many survive on secondary and goods lines.

▲ Although the principles of signalling had been standardized by the 1920s, there was still room for local variations, usually with the aim of increasing visibility. Small-scale, low-level repeaters were not uncommon, such as this group at Tring, Hertfordshire, photographed in the 1930s.

◄ A classic and once universal railway scene: the signalman stands at his door and surveys his domain, which included the paired home and distant signals in the foreground.

▶ Semaphore signals are essentially Victorian technology, but they survive on some secondary lines. This group controlled the junction with the Ely docks branch. They were photographed in 1989.

▼ The most impressive sight in signal terms at any major station used to be the great gantry spanning the platforms and loaded with semaphore signals to control every track. This example, partly hidden by the smoke from the departing Bournemouth train in June 1963, was at Southampton.

◀ Despite constant improvements and moves towards standardization, many old or unusual semaphore signals survived, in many cases reflecting the individuality of the pre-Grouping era. This one was photographed at Cheam, Surrey, in 1937.

▲ On some single lines, such as the Hayling branch, signals faced both ways. Despite all the smoke, the train was unlikely to exceed the 20mph limit.

▼ The most impressive signal gantries were not necessarily at the largest stations. This magnificent example was at Alnwick, Northumberland, seen here controlling the arrival of the passenger train from Alnmouth, hauled by class J39 no. 64897.

► In 1968 steam and diesel meet either side of Preston's massive signal gantry.

◄ An ancient signal surviving on an ancient railway, photographed in 1962 near Whimsey Halt on the Forest of Dean line to Bullo Pill. The embankment behind used to carry the Severn & Wye line to Cinderford, closed in 1958.

► While signals were meant, for safety reasons, to be all the same, there were, in fact, infinite variations, determined often by the setting. Another mark of individuality was the iron or wood finial, which often had defined company characteristics.

▲ In 1967 a football special, under the control of a Britannia class 4-6-2, no. 70010, 'Owen Glendower', races towards Mallerstang signal box while the signal, on a post heightened for visibility, indicates an approaching train.

LOST LIVERIES

One of the unexpected fruits of railway privatization has been the proliferation of constantly changing train liveries. As a result, stations are now as colourful as they were in the Victorian and pre-Grouping eras. Distinctive locomotive and carriage colour schemes developed from the 1840s as the various railway companies, increasingly aware of the need for a corporate image, opened their own workshops. Liveries were usually determined by the company engineers, who specified their colours in great detail. Strangely, many companies had separate colour schemes for locomotives and carriages, thereby adding to the visual diversity at major stations. For example, in this period, Carlisle Citadel station was served by seven separate railway companies, so at busy times the platforms must have been an explosion of colour. The 1923 Grouping brought a degree of standardization, and some schemes from this time survived the process of nationalization. During the first three decades of its existence, British Railways used three major liveries, the last of which was predominantly blue.

▲ In the Edwardian era large numbers of colourful postcards captured the great variety of locomotive liveries. This 4-4-2 tank engine displays the grey-blue livery of the London, Tilbury & Southend Railway in use in about 1910, a change from the earlier green.

◄ There were many tones of blue to be seen around the network, but one of the most memorable was the deep blue of the Great Eastern Railway. This 4-4-0 locomotive, built at Stratford works in 1910, shows the elaborate lining out that was typical of these schemes.

◄ This 4-4-0 express locomotive was built at the Midland Railway's Derby works in 1907. The tone of red favoured by the Midland was distinctive and justifiably famous. Unusually among railway companies of that era, the Midland painted its carriages the same colour as its locomotives.

► Green was always the favourite colour for locomotives but there were many variations. This is the Great Northern's version, shown on a late-Victorian 4-2-2 locomotive.

◄ Another tone of green was chosen by the London & South Western Railway, displayed here on a Urie class H15 4-6-0 express locomotive, built at Eastleigh works in 1914.

► A small company with a limited network, the North Staffordshire Railway enjoyed a reputation that belied its size and it took great pride in the appearance of its trains. Locomotives were painted a deep maroon, such as this 4-4-0 built at their works in Stoke in 1910.

SOUTHERN
ENGLAND

LOST & FOUND

FOOTPATHS, OFFICIAL OR UNOFFICIAL, are the best way to see old railways. This one on the Isle of Wight leads towards Wroxall and the downs above Ventnor.

△ OLD RAILWAYS survive most often as tracks used by farmers for access to their fields, and for the dumping of old farm machinery. This example is on the former Hawkhurst branch in Kent.

◁ SURVIVAL IS ARBITRARY. Little remains of the Westerham branch in Kent, which closed in 1961. Yet, near Dunton Green, bits of the concrete branch platform and a signal cable wheel lurk in the undergrowth.

▷ A PARTICULARLY ATTRACTIVE railway walk is along the Meon valley in Hampshire. Plenty of railway reminders remain, such as this bridge across the Meon at Soberton.

ISLE OF WIGHT

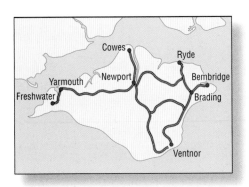

Railways on the Isle of Wight were first proposed in the 1840s but it was not until 1862 that the island's first line, the Cowes & Newport Railway, was actually opened. Over the next thirty-eight years other lines arrived, built by a bewildering number of small and independent companies, including the Ryde & Newport, the Isle of Wight (Newport Junction), the Freshwater, Yarmouth & Newport, the Newport, Godshill & St Lawrence and the Brading Harbour Improvement. Some thrived, some had financial difficulties. In the end they were all absorbed into two companies, the larger of which, Isle of Wight Central, operated a 28-mile network. The result of all this was that the island was remarkably well served by its 55-mile railway network, with passenger and freight services to most major, and many minor, places and rail-served harbours at Bembridge and on the Medina near Cowes. Ventnor had two stations, and Ryde three. Like the Isle of Wight itself, the railways were a microcosm of Victorian England, and this atmosphere was maintained well into the 20th century, and through periods of operation by the Southern Railway and ultimately British Railways. The sense of past pleasures was underlined by the long-established habit of sending to the island ancient locomotives and rolling stock discarded by the mainland's railways, with the result that some locomotives from the 1860s were still at work in the 1930s.

In the pre-car age, the railways thrived but by the 1950s competition, for passengers and freight, was taking its toll. First to close, in September 1952, was the line from Ventnor West to Merstone. Soon, the lines from Brading to Bembridge, from Newport to Freshwater and from Newport to Sandown followed. In 1966 the rest of the network disappeared, though a year later the section from Ryde Pier Head to Shanklin was reopened, having been electrified for operation by retired London tube trains. A further section, from Wootton to Smallbrook Junction,

▲ Even in August 1965 Ventnor's station, seen here from above the entrance to the tunnel, was still a busy place, with a long train about to depart for Ryde. Today, the station site is an industrial estate.

▼ It is the summer of 1966 and closure is round the corner, but services must still run. At Ryde Pier Head, two of the island's distinctive locomotives rest between duties: no. 27 'Merstone' takes water, while no. 16 'Ventnor' sits in platform 1.

► Newport was the hub of the network, and its most distinctive feature was the viaduct that carried the trains across the Medina and into the town. This was frequently photographed from the road below but this more unusual view is taken from the carriage window.

▼ In an image that captures the special atmosphere of the island's railways, the signals are set and the train is ready to depart from Brading, in the early 1960s.

is now a preserved line. Elsewhere, though much has vanished for ever, there is still plenty to be seen, particularly in rural areas. Between Shanklin and Wroxall, and between Yarmouth and Freshwater, the trackbed is a footpath and, in the latter case, a cycletrack. Another cycleway goes through Merstone Junction towards Newport. For the dedicated lost railway hunter, there are hidden sections of overgrown trackbed and surviving bridges between Yarmouth and Newport, while from St Helens to Bembridge a path marks the route of the railway. Another walkable section is between Newport and Wootton, with Whippingham station still there as a private house. Other stations and crossing-keeper's cottages have become private houses, for example at Whitwell and Alverstone. However, with few significant engineering features to mark its routes, much of the railway has simply gone back into the landscape. Hardest to trace is the southern section of the line from Ventnor West to Merstone, although the dramatic quarry that housed Ventnor's main station is still there, along with the boarded-up entrance to the long tunnel underneath St Boniface Down. Today, the history of the island's railways is mostly told by pleasant walks, good views and occasional relics.

▲ The old route of the railway from Yarmouth station – which survives, with its platform – to the outskirts of Freshwater has long been a footpath, cycleway and occasional bridleway. This wooded section is at the Freshwater end.

▲ ► Freshwater, opened in 1889, was the end of the line and the most westerly station on the network. From the early days, it catered for tourist traffic, as the Edwardian postcard above indicates, with carriages waiting to take passengers to Alum Bay. On the right, in a scene from about 1950, no. 33 'Bembridge' has just arrived with a trainload of well-dressed holidaymakers.

▼ From Yarmouth station the railway ran alongside the tidal estuary of the Yar on a low embankment, with fine views to the west. Today, walkers and cyclists can enjoy these from a well-maintained trackbed path.

◄ The branch to Bembridge, built originally to serve the harbour, was closed in 1953 and much has gone. However, the route of the railway can still be followed from St Helens station, now a private house, to the outskirts of Bembridge, flanking the broad expanse of Bembridge harbour, to the right of the old trackbed in this picture.

◄ Even on well-trodden paths there are railway relics to be found. This old Southern Railway gate used to guard a farmtrack crossing on the line north of Wroxall. Today this is a pleasant walk, partly through woods and partly on an embankment with fine views towards Wroxall and the downs beyond.

► The line from Wootton to Smallbrook is alive and well as the Isle of Wight Steam Railway. From Wootton westwards to Newport, however, it is a different story. A section near Whippingham is a footpath but elsewhere the remains are hidden and impenetrable. This broken bridge is deep in woods near Wootton Common.

► The least-used part of the island's network was the line from Merstone Junction south to Ventnor West. It was completed in 1900 by the Newport, Godshill & St Lawrence Railway. It soon went bankrupt, and was finally closed in 1953. This 1930s view of Whitwell station shows the rural nature of this remote railway. The man on the platform may have a long wait.

HAVANT TO HAYLING ISLAND

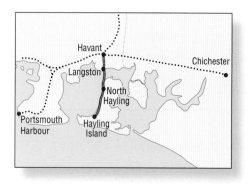

▲ Shoppers leave the Hayling train after its arrival in the bay platform at Havant station in the 1950s. The little Terrier locomotive prepares to run round the train.

Havant has always been an important junction and the meeting point of several lines. The years following its opening in 1847 were overshadowed by aggressive competition between the two great rivals, the London & South Western and the London, Brighton & South Coast. Eventually, in 1859, a modus vivendi was reached and the station and its mainline traffic soon expanded. A further addition to the station complex was the arrival in 1867 of the Hayling Railway. Work on this independent line had started in 1863 but constant financial problems delayed the completion of the 4-mile branch. Even when it was finally opened, problems continued: the company had no money for rolling stock, so for the first four years of the railway's life services were operated by the contractor who had built it, using his own locomotives and ancient carriages hired from the London & South Western. Subsequently the railway was leased to the London, Brighton & South Coast, but it remained independently owned until it was absorbed into the Southern Railway in 1923. Havant station was rebuilt in the 1880s and the 1930s.

In its heyday the Hayling Railway was a busy holiday route, with up to four trains an hour in the height of summer, and in its later life it became famous among railway enthusiasts as one of the last regular habitats of the tiny class AIX tank locomotives, popularly known as Terriers. These primarily Victorian engines, the oldest of which dated back to the 1870s, worked the line until its closure in November 1963. Anything else would have been too heavy for the weak wooden bridge across Langstone Harbour.

▲ The most popular view of the Hayling branch was one with the train crossing the Langstone viaduct, preferably at sunset. This photograph is a good example, and it shows well the diminutive size of the Terrier tank engines.

▼ The viaduct's concrete supports survive to mark the route, along with the famous signal, a monument to the line. The former route across the island, between North Hayling and Hayling Island stations, is a public cycleway and footpath known as the Hayling Billy Trail.

▼ With the low-lying and flowery embankment stretching ahead towards Havant, the driver of a rather grimy Terrier has left the cab to do something to the coal bunker – or perhaps just to check the amount of coal remaining.

▼ Two ill-assorted old carriages and a tired Terrier, no. 32670, make up a typical Hayling Island train as it approaches the basic timber station at North Hayling. Driver and guard look ahead but there are no passengers to be seen.

▼ There is no one around but bicycles lean against the classic SR cream-and-green shed and, across the line, someone has been having a bit of a clear-out. It is a quiet day at South Hayling, or Hayling Island as it was also known, the end of the branch. And the signals agree that nothing is happening.

"HAYLING BILLY"

Weight : 28 tons 5 cwt.
Driving Wheel Diameter: 4' 0"
Tractive Effect at 85% B.P. — 10,695 lbs.
Cylinders : 14⅜" x 20"
Valve Gear: Stephenson
Boiler Pressure : 150 lbs. sq. in.

One of the famous 0-6-0T Class A1X Brighton Terriers known locally and affectionately as 'Hayling Billies'.

This was one of a class of 50 designed by William Stroudley, Locomotive Superintendent of the London, Brighton and South Coast Railway, built at the Brighton works in 1876, and put into service in January 1877 as 'No. 46 Newington'.

It was sold in 1903 to the London and South Western Railway and then in 1913 transferred to the Isle of Wight in the service of the Freshwater, Yarmouth and Newport Railway.

In 1923 under the railway companies grouping, it was absorbed into the service of the Southern Railway, re-boilered and given the name "Freshwater".

Upon nationalisation it returned to the mainland in 1949 and was re-numbered BR 32646, based at Fratton and used on the Havant-Hayling line until the closure on 2nd November 1963.

The last run under steam was made on 13th May 1966 and it is now restored in the original "Scotch Green" livery of William Stroudley.

▲ After the line closed, Hayling Billy, aka former London, Brighton & South Coast Terrier no. 46, 'Newington' of 1876 and latterly BR 32646, was restored to its original colours and displayed for a while outside the Hayling Billy pub at Elm Grove.

LONGMOOR MILITARY RAILWAY

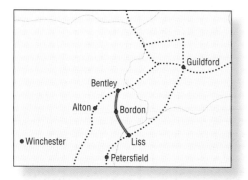

The Victorian army appreciated the strategic value of railways. Engineers, for example, were given specialist training in railway work for the Sudan and Egyptian campaigns. Training carried on at Woolwich Arsenal and elsewhere until 1905, when the Woolmer Instructional Military Railway was set up in Hampshire to train military engineers in all aspects of railway construction, operation and management. In 1935 this became the Longmoor Military Railway. Running from a branch from Bentley, near Alton, to Liss on the Petersfield line, this was a complete railway network, serving camps, firing ranges, training areas, workshops and depots. There were thirteen intermediate stations and miles of sidings, many of which were vital in the build-up to D-Day in 1944.

In later years Longmoor was famous for its annual open day. The railway closed in 1969 and today there is little to be seen, with much of the route still on army land. The southern section is a footpath, the Royal Woolmer Way.

▲ Bordon Camp was a massive military base, served by the Longmoor Railway and by the LSWR branch from Bentley (closed to passengers in 1957). This card shows the Wesleyan Soldiers' Home at Bordon, c.1910.

▼ Finding the remains of the Longmoor Railway is hard as much is still on army land. Hidden in the woods near Bordon are concrete buffers, the remains of long sidings where trains were hidden prior to D-Day.

▼ Longmoor Camp itself is to the south of Bordon. The route of the old line towards Longmoor is popular with walkers and cyclists.

LONGMOOR MILITARY RAILWAY
OPEN DAY - 3rd JUNE, 1967
Valid for travel between LISS,
LONGMOOR DOWNS & OAKHANGER
and via HOLLYWATER LOOP
For conditions see over
Williamson, Ticket Printer. Ashton-u-Lyne
0621 0621

▼ The most accessible part of the former railway today is the section north of Liss, part of which is now the Royal Woolmer Way. Among the surviving relics to be seen is this bridge over a stream, dramatically hidden in woods, and clearly built to carry heavy trains.

▲ Longmoor open days were popular events each year, with trains from the railway's unusual fleet on show, including 'Gordon', the famous WD 2-10-0 locomotive. This shows an early 1960s open day.

LOST STATIONS: SOUTHERN ENGLAND

The south of England was the region least affected by the closure programmes of the 1960s, mainly because so much of the network was commuter-based and therefore carried regular heavy passenger traffic. However, there was plenty of duplication in the network, and this is what Dr Beeching addressed primarily, along with uneconomical rural routes and branch lines. Major losses occurred around Alton, East Grinstead and Lewes, notably the by then little-used cross-country connecting lines. The Isle of Wight's network was largely obliterated and branchline closures included Grain, Westerham, Hawkhurst and Dungeness. There had, of course, been earlier closures, for example the Selsey, Lee-on-the-Solent, Hythe and Sandgate, and Leysdown lines. Another early loss had been the famous Canterbury & Whitstable Railway, whose history pre-dated the Liverpool & Manchester. Land pressures and values in the South have meant that many closed lines have largely vanished, along with hundreds of stations. Here are memories of some major and minor stations in the region, mostly lost for ever.

◄ In 1894 a short branch to Lee-on-the-Solent was opened from Fort Brockhurst on the Gosport line. Never financially viable, it was an early closure candidate, and passenger services ended in 1931. Here, the little station and the train wait in vain for traffic.

▼ Barcombe was a station on the line from East Grinstead to Lewes, part of which is now the Bluebell Railway. Passenger services went early, in 1958, but freight continued for a while.

▲ Southampton's original terminus, or docks, station was a splendid classical building designed by Sir William Tite and completed in 1840. Seen here in 1918, it remained in use until 1966. A listed building, it survives but not as a station.

▲ Brookland Halt was the only intermediate station on the branch from Appledore to New Romney and Dungeness, opened in the 1890s. In November 1966, a few months before closure, a few passengers could still admire the old South Eastern Railway lamp.

▶ The Hundred of Manhood & Selsey Railway completed its line south from Chichester to Selsey in 1897. Holiday traffic was its mainstay and it later became part of Colonel Stephens's empire, before closing in January 1935. Selsey was one of ten stations.

▼ Petworth was a station on the cross-country line from Petersfield to Pulborough. This lost its passenger service in 1955 but Petworth station lived on, as this 1979 photograph shows. It is now a hotel.

LOST JOURNEY: VENTNOR TO TENTERDEN

This slow and laborious journey across southern England started and finished with idiosyncratic minor railways, the Isle of Wight network and the Kent & East Sussex line. In between was a sea crossing, a mainline railway along the south coast and a cross-country route, with plenty of time to explore Tunbridge Wells. In the pre-car age, such journeys would have been commonplace for people going on holiday, visiting family or friends or travelling for work reasons. In those days, such a journey, taking nearly 12 hours, would have been quite acceptable, for the railway's extensive network across Hampshire, Sussex and Kent had made the region accessible to all. Today it would be impossible. Only a fragment of the Isle of Wight's railways exists, though the ferry to Portsmouth is still quick and frequent. The main line from Portsmouth to Brighton is much the same, but to travel from Brighton to Tunbridge Wells today would involve a major detour via St Leonards. The line from Tunbridge Wells to Robertsbridge is still there, but the old Kent & East Sussex vanished years ago. However, part of the route is now a preserved line, so Tenterden Town is a station once more, though isolated from the main network.

TIMETABLE	
Ventnor..................................	7.40am
Ryde Pier Head....................	8.29am
Ship..	8.35–9.05am
Portsmouth Harbour.........	10.08am
Brighton...............................	11.36am
Change	
Brighton...............................	12.05pm
Tunbridge Wells West........	1.20pm
Walk to	
Tunbridge Wells Central	
Tunbridge Wells Central	3.48pm
Robertbridge.........................	4.23pm
Change	
Robertsbridge......................	5.50pm
Tenterden Town...................	6.30pm

VENTNOR FROM THE AIR.

Aerofilms Series.

◄ VENTNOR IS SET ON steep hills, with its many hotels – then as now – overlooking the beach, which in this 1950s aerial view is crowded. There were two stations: a minor one at Ventnor West, on the old line to Newport via Merstone, and the main station, the start of this journey, which was off the postcard to the right.

Worthing

Chichester

PORTSMOUTH

Ryde Pier Head

VENTNOR

H.M.S Victory, Portsmouth

► IN THE EDWARDIAN era, HMS *Victory* was still afloat in Portsmouth harbour, and was a highlight of the journey on the paddle steamer from Ryde. Sailing between Ryde Pier Head and Portsmouth Harbour, the ship was a direct link between two seaside stations built out over the water.

Brighton Station

WARE EMPORIUM

▲ BRIGHTON STATION lies high above the town, a splendid seaside terminus. It was opened in 1841 and then extensively enlarged and rebuilt in the 1880s. This card shows how it looked in about 1910 and it looks much the same today, with plenty of decorative ironwork inside and out. The sea is about 15 minutes' walk away, but on this journey there was only time for a coffee at the station refreshment room.

TUNBRIDGE WELLS

▲ TUNBRIDGE WELLS'S two stations, West and Central, were some way apart, but on this journey there was plenty of time for the walk between them, as well as for lunch and a visit to the famous shop in the Pantiles that sold Tunbridge Ware, the delicate inlaid woodwork associated with the town.

BRIGHTON   Lewes

TENTERDEN

ROBERTSBRIDGE

▲ A LOCAL PAUSES AT ROBERTSBRIDGE on a sunny day in the 1930s. Some of the passengers would no doubt be following the sign and changing for the eccentric Kent & East Sussex Light Railway, then part of Colonel Stephens's empire.

▶ TENTERDEN IS A FAMOUSLY picturesque town, spread around a large central green. In this 1920s postcard from a painting by AH Quintin, a farm cart adds to the charm of the scene.

RAILWAY WORKS

T he first works dedicated to the making of railway locomotives and equipment was set up by George and Robert Stephenson in 1823. Others quickly followed as railway mania gripped the nation, and many of the great names were in business by the 1860s, including Hawthorn, Kitson, Manning Wardle, Hunslet, Beyer Peacock and Barclay. These, and others, formed the basis of a large private railway locomotive and vehicle building business that continued to develop through the latter part of the 19th century and much of the 20th, thanks in part to a thriving export market. The largest and probably the best known was the North British Locomotive Company, formed from mergers in Glasgow in 1903. Developing in parallel were the works set up by the larger railway companies, initially for maintenance but from the 1840s for the manufacture of locomotives and rolling stock. In the end, there were about thirty works in Britain in which railway companies built their own locomotives. In this list are the familiar names Eastleigh, Ashford, Swindon, Crewe, Derby, Doncaster, Darlington and St Rollox, along with many lesser-known places, for example Kilmarnock, Stoke-on-Trent and Melton Constable. At its peak, the British railway industry was making about 2,000 locomotives a year. The 1923 Grouping and the subsequent formation of British Railways greatly reduced the number of railway works. In 1970 British Rail Engineering Limited was formed and by 1988 the only major building works still active were Crewe and Derby.

▲ The Midland Railway's works at Derby, established from 1873, is one of the best-known in Britain, and one of the few still in operation. This view shows the erecting shop in LMS days.

▲ Swindon works was set up by the GWR from 1841, turning a Wiltshire village into a major industrial town. The first locomotive was built in 1846 and the last, 'Evening Star', in 1960. This 1959 view shows the powerful GWR 2-8-0 7F 4700 class no. 4700 being overhauled. The works closed in 1986, though some buildings remain. The Railway Village is a conservation area.

▼ The London, Brighton & South Coast Railway's Brighton works opened in 1852 and by 1903 it gave employment to 6 per cent of the town. Later, carriages and wagons were built at Lancing, but Brighton made locomotives until 1958.

▲ WG Bagnall began to build locomotives at Stafford in 1876 and grew to become a major independent manufacturer, specializing later in industrial locomotives. This view shows their Castle works.

TUNNELS

Tunnels are one of the most remarkable features of the railway age, representing as they do great engineering and astonishing feats of construction. Until the 1860s, railway engineers used the tunnelling technology of the 18th-century canal age, and every one was built by hand. The earliest railways, the Canterbury & Whitstable, the Liverpool & Manchester and the Leicester & Swannington, had tunnels on their routes, and the rapid expansion of the network brought hundreds more into being. In the end, there were about 1,060 tunnels in Britain, the longest of which is the one under the Severn, whose bore, 4 miles 628yd long, took fourteen years to build. Another eight are over 2 miles long. Fifty are over a mile long. The deepest is Cowburn in Derbyshire, 875ft below the surface. The closing of lines inevitably resulted in many tunnels going out of use, but the durability of their structure meant that most survived. A few have been given new lives, as shooting ranges, for storage, and for the cultivation of mushrooms, and some have been taken over by bats and are, as a result, protected. Many have been sealed up and are inaccessible, but plenty remain open and can be explored by walkers and railway enthusiasts. Some are even on official footpaths and cycle routes. There is something particularly appealing about exploring a disused railway tunnel – a sense of history, an appreciation of the efforts of the men who built it, and the sheer excitement of the voyage through the dark.

▲ In 1956 a local stopping train makes its way through Miller's Dale, following the old Midland Railway's line through the Derbyshire hills, a route notable for viaducts and tunnels. The line closed in 1968.

▶ In an image that captures totally the lure of the abandoned tunnel, three children pose below the ancient stone portal of Haie Hill tunnel, in the Forest of Dean, in August 1967, just a couple of weeks after the line's closure.

▼ Catesby tunnel was completed in 1897, on the Great Central's route through Northamptonshire. Over a mile long, the tunnel was closed with much of the former GCR route in 1966. The elegant engineering-brick portals have since been sealed up.

▶ In tunnel terms, few names are more famous than Woodhead. Carved through the Pennines on the line between Sheffield and Manchester, the first tunnel, more than 3 miles long, was one of the great epics of early railway history. Completed in 1845, it was followed by a second, parallel tunnel in 1852. Just over a century later, both these single-track tunnels were replaced by a massive new bore, 27ft wide and 20ft high. Here, a freight train enters one of the castellated portals of the old tunnels. The whole route was closed in 1981, but reopening remains a possibility.

▼ A long-abandoned tunnel and its approach cutting, overgrown and hidden in woods, is often an evocative sight, hinting at closure centuries rather than decades ago. This one is near the site of Lydbrook Junction, in the Forest of Dean.

▶ A group of serious-looking and surprisingly well-dressed enthusiasts emerge from the mouth of Glenfield tunnel, on the Barrhead-to-Paisley line, west of Glasgow. Nearly everyone has a tie and a smart haircut. The only woman present is well to the rear. The line closed in 1965.

▼ Ventnor, at the end of the line from Ryde, was an unusual station on the southern shore of the Isle of Wight. It was set into a vast excavated area that looked like a quarry, and the approach was through a long tunnel under St Boniface Down. Emerging trains came straight to the platforms, surrounded by smoke and steam, as can be seen here. The station site and the tunnel, now bricked up, survive.

OVERGROUND & UNDERGROUND

A feature of the late Victorian period was the rapid expansion of public transport in towns and cities. From the 1890s electric tramways were being built all over Britain and in London and Glasgow electric underground railways were running in deep bored tunnels while Queen Victoria was still on the throne. The older cut and cover lines had been built from the 1860s, but deep tunnelling and electric power represented the new technology. The London underground was to be greatly expanded during the Edwardian period, with much of the modern network in the centre of London in place before World War I. In the United States and France there was a preference for elevated urban railways, but in Britain only Liverpool took this route in any significant way with the building from 1893 of the first 6 miles of the Liverpool Overhead Railway.

Overhead Railway
Liverpool.

▲ The Liverpool Overhead Railway was the first electric urban system in the world and the first with automated signalling. These two photographs, taken in 1910, show the relationship between the railway and Liverpool's extensive docks. It was built 16ft above street level to facilitate access to the docks and to transport the thousands who worked there. The original line, from Dingle to Seaforth, had been extended by then to meet the Lancashie & Yorkshire lines to Southport and Ormskirk. Electric power was used to reduce the risk of fire in the warehouses.

◄ This card, postmarked 1910, shows the popularity of the Overhead Railway, and the efficient service it offered. Never part of the nationalized network, it remained in use until 1956.

► Underground railway companies had many specialized vehicles to carry out maintenance at night or when the system was closed to the public. This Edwardian Central London promotional card shows a tunnel-whitewashing train, something unimaginable on today's London underground network.

► Nowadays dogs travel free on the London underground.

► Many London underground stations have changed their names. This is an Edwardian view of the entrance to Post Office station, on the Central London Railway, now St Paul's station, on the Central Line.

▼ The Metropolitan was an independent railway with a large suburban network. It had freight and parcels facilities and even, on some services, Pullman cars. Electrified from 1905, it had distinctive locomotives and carriages, yet became a part of the London Transport underground network from 1933, while retaining its look and identity. Today it is just the Metropolitan line.

▲ This 1908 map, geographical rather than diagrammatic, shows much of the central London underground network in place and is therefore recognizable today. However, there have been changes. At least four stations on the map, Brompton Road, Down Street, York Road and Castle Road, no longer exist. Others have been renamed: Dover Street is now called Green Park, Great Central is Marylebone, Gillespie Road is Arsenal, Euston Road is Warren Street, British Museum is Holborn.

A NEW LEASE OF LIFE

When a railway carriage comes to the end of its life, the final resting place is usually the scrapyard. The chassis and running gear may be reused but the body is broken up or burned. It was ever thus. However, railway companies have always been aware that carriage bodies can be useful, so there is a long tradition of using them as stores, mess rooms, dormitories and even station waiting rooms. It has also been known for decades that a railway carriage can be turned into an adequate home. This practice was at its peak in the 1920s, when a severe housing shortage after World War I coincided with the decision, taken for safety reasons largely as a result of the disaster at Quintinshill in 1915, to do away with wooden-bodied carriages. The process was helped by the lack of planning laws and by the railway companies' willingness to sell off redundant vehicles. Old carriages appeared in fields all over Britain, usually in ones or twos but sometimes in colonies, with famous examples at Shoreham and Selsey, in Sussex, and Dungeness, in Kent. Today only a small number of carriage homes survive, and time, weather and land values ensure that the number diminishes each year. A very few have been rescued after years of use as living accommodation and are back at work on preserved lines.

▲ A family poses proudly outside its carriage home in the 1930s. This example, known as Brockley, was brought to Worth Matravers, in Dorset, in 1927, pulled to its site by teams of horses.

▲ There were many uses to which an old railway carriage could be put, apart from living accommodation. This one found a new life as a school annexe in Ackworth, to the east of Wakefield, in Yorkshire.

▼ This ex-LNER carriage, with several others, enjoyed for some years a new life on a siding at Newton Abbot, in Devon, as offices for the publishers of this book, David & Charles.

► After many years away from the rails, this carriage, a rare survivor from the Jersey Eastern Railway, was rescued in the 1960s and transported to a new life in the Jersey Motor Museum. At this point the doors were still labelled 'Guard', 'Luggage', 'First', 'Second' and 'Second'.

▼ A famous example of carriage reuse was to be seen for some years at Gatehouse of Fleet, in Dumfries & Galloway, where this long clerestory vehicle was in service as a church.

► On many rural and branch lines, railway companies saved money by using carriage bodies as waiting rooms. This one was at Cutler's Green Halt, on the Thaxted branch, in Essex.

▲ Carriage cottages do still survive in
surprising locations. This example, still
recognizable despite extensive additions,
is on a main road in South Wootton, near
King's Lynn, in Norfolk. Maybe its active life
was on the line to Hunstanton.

▶ Many old carriages extended their lives as
camping coaches. In 1968 this former SE&CR
royal saloon was one such at Glenfinnan, on
the Fort William-to-Mallaig line.

▼Another survivor lives on as a summer house in a private garden near
Lessingham, not far from the Norfolk coast. Today, it is a long way from any
railway but when it arrived decades ago it probably came from Stalham, a
couple of miles away and then on the M&GN's Cromer-to-Yarmouth line.

▲ The family poses with the newly arrived carriages, delivered by horse-drawn carts.

▲ The two bodies are placed side by side on the acre plot purchased for the new house.

▲ Construction starts of the roof that will span the two carriages.

Carriage cottages may survive, but their history is often lost. It is, therefore, a rare treat to be able to tell the full story of one that did not get away. The principle was that the railway company would sell the carriage body, and the price included its transport to a station of the buyer's choice. Transport from that station or goods yard to the site was the buyer's responsibility. In August 1923 this family took delivery of two old carriage bodies from the Southern Railway which, as the original invoice shows, was using up old LSWR stationery. The price for the two was £39. Remarkably, the house that was then built from these carriages is still owned by the same family, along with the photographs that document the arrival of the carriages and their conversion into a substantial holiday home.

▲ With the house finished, the carriages have almost disappeared. This survives unchanged.

▲ By 1924 the holiday home was in use, as this view of the living room shows.

... MORE LOST LIVERIES

TEN WHEELED TANK LOCOMOTIVE. M.&G.N.R.

◀ An unusual colour was the light brown chosen by the Midland & Great Northern Junction Railway, shown here on a 4-4-2 tank built at the company's Melton Constable woarks in 1904.

▼ The Caledonian's blue was justly famous, and rather brighter than this card suggests. It is shown here on a 4-6-0 express locomotive built at the St Rollox works in 1913.

▼ Many Victorian railways preferred practical black, and this tradition was maintained by the LMS, as seen on this class 4P 2-6-4 engine, and subsequently by British Railways.

LPC/74   L.M.S. class " 4P " parallel boiler 2-6-4T No. 2313

STROUDLEY'S FOUR COUPLED EXPRESS, L.B. & S.C.R.

▶ William Stroudley was the great locomotive engineer for the London, Brighton & South Coast Railway, and he chose the distinctive mustard yellow, shown here on one of his famous Gladstone 0-4-2 engines.

◄ Unlike its famous rival, the Caledonian, the Highland Railway chose a sombre but nevertheless elegant colour scheme for its locomotives. This is 'Murthly Castle', a Drummond 4-6-0 built in 1900.

► The Furness Railway had an extensive Cumbrian network, which pioneered tourist traffic. It was famous for its smart red locomotives and blue-and-cream carriages, seen here on a Lake District Express in about 1910.

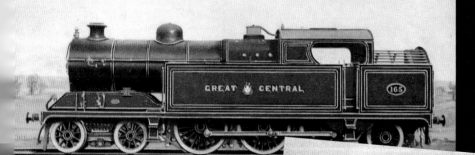

◄ The Great Central's locomotives combined power with elegance. This large 4-6-2 tank engine, smart in its green livery with rich detailing, was built at the company's works at Gorton in 1911 to the designs of JG Robinson.

► One of the individual and independently minded railways was the Somerset & Dorset Joint, whose dark blue scheme is shown here on one of their typical 4-4-0 locomotives.

Somerset and Dorset Joint Railway – No. 77 Express Engine.

SIGNAL BOXES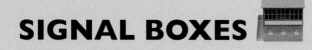

T hough not yet extinct, the signal box is, thanks to modern electronics, an endangered species. Only a few hundred survive from the many thousands that used to exist. It is hard to imagine that something so close to the heart of railway history, and so familiar, will eventually disappear from the national network. In due course the signal box will follow the steam locomotive into that Jurassic Park of the railway, the preserved line. The signal box emerged in the 1860s, with the development of interlocking machinery that connected the control of signals and points, and then spread steadily over the network. The typical box was a two-storey structure, with the machinery on the ground floor, housed in brick or stone, and the levers and working space in the upper storey, which was usually made from wood. In principle, as they performed identical functions, all signal boxes could be the same. In practice, there was an infinite variety, and therein lay the box's enduring appeal. There was a huge range of sizes, shapes and settings, and great diversity of styles, many of which made the most of decorative timberwork. Bargeboarding, fretwork, finials, unusual window detailing, all played a part as railway companies relished the challenge of making individual something mundane and apparently predictable. There are echoes of fashionable architectural styles, from Gothic to Art Deco. Signalmen needed good all-round vision, a practical working space and creature comforts such as a stove, a cooker and, in later years, a lavatory.

▲ Firsby North, a box on the line between Boston and Louth, was looking a bit past its best in 1980. A typical timber-upper and brick-lower box, with decorative woodwork, it still boasted its nameboard and fire-buckets.

▼ Signalmen, like all railway staff, used standard codes for all telegraph communication. This 1958 edition gives the meaning of codes such as Ape, Bobol, Earwig, Hux, Pike, Slog, Tiber, Watty and Zest.

▼ When photographed in 1984, Bardon Hill box, near Coalville, in Leicestershire, was a classic, in a remarkable state of repair, and still with its original nameboard. In the old days, signal boxes were often well kept, mainly because they were manned all the time.

BARDON HILL

BRITISH TRANSPORT COMMISSION

BRITISH RAILWAYS

STANDARD CODES
FOR
TELEGRAMS

1st July, 1958

▼ At Barton Street Junction by Gloucester's Eastgate station the box was set high on the gantry like a crow's nest, to ensure good visibility for the signalmen. Such arrangements were not unusual. Despite the functional nature of its position, the box still has decorative window frames and a roof finial.

BARTON STREET JUNCTION

London Midland and Scottish Railway Company.

CODE OF RINGS FOR FOG BELL

BETWEEN

SIGNAL BOX & STATION MASTER'S HOUSE

AT

PLUMPTON.

									RINGS.
Attention Signal	...	...	...	...	...	...	...	...	1
Lampman required	...	...	...	...	...	...	...	...	2
Fogsignalmen required	...	...	...	...	...	...	...	...	3
Assistance or Station Master required	...	...	...	...	...	...			4
Testing Bell Signal	...	...	...	...	...	...	...	...	16

The Attention Signal must be sent before any of the above codes are given, and such signal must be repeated at short intervals until replied to. Each code must be acknowledged by repetition to show that it is correctly understood, and if incorrectly repeated, must be given again until a correct reply is received.

Should any accident or obstruction occur, rendering assistance necessary, or should the Station Master be required, the Signalman will give 4 rings, and the Station Master must at once proceed to the Signal Box.

The Station Master must give the Testing Signal.

Any failure of the electric bell must be at once reported to the Electrical Department.

BY ORDER

of the

September, 1929.   CHIEF GENERAL SUPERINTENDENT.

◄ While much of the Isle of Wight's railway system was quiet and rural, Newport, at the network's heart, was a busy place. This box, with its pretty bargeboarding, controlled an important group of signals and points.

► When lines closed, signal boxes were generally stripped of their machinery and fittings but the buildings often remained, to be gradually destroyed by weather and vandals. This is the former box at St Briavels & Llandogo, on the Chepstow-to-Monmouth line, originally a handsome stone-built structure. As can be seen, the crossing gates had also survived in February 1966, when this photograph was taken.

▼ In its heyday, Newton Abbot, Devon, was a major interchange station, handling busy passenger and goods traffic for both main and branch lines. The signal box was, therefore, a substantial building, and surprisingly large for one built from wood. The state of the box in 1984 reflects the station's relative decline since the 1960s.

▲ Boxes came in all shapes and sizes and the smaller ones often controlled just a level crossing or a few sets of points. The delightfully named Chapel of Ease Crossing was by the Duffryn Yard in Port Talbot. In September 1963, this dedicated enthusiast has obviously carried out an inspection.

▲ Roxton was a small station on the line between Market Drayton and Wellington. Clearly kept in good order, the box featured an unusual style of timber construction.

▼ By 1973 the little Thorp Hall box was well past its best and was even looking rather derelict. Yet there are plenty of signs of activity and two railwaymen can be seen inside – as well as tea-making equipment, an essential part of signal-box life.

WALES

LOST & FOUND

A RAILWAY IN A SPECTACULAR setting: the old GWR line from Blaenau Ffestiniog towards Bala. Part of it was kept open to service Trawsfynydd power station.

◀ THINGS THAT SURVIVE by chance become interesting with time, and are even preserved, such as remains of the crossing gates at Glogue, on the Cardigan branch, now carefully painted.

▲ THE ANGLESEY BRANCH to Red Wharf Bay closed in 1930, yet there are still traces to be found, such as this short stretch of trackbed through the wood.

◀ WINTER IS A GOOD TIME for exploring old railways, as the embankments are more visible. The Newcastle Emlyn branch followed river valleys, seen here in fields beside the Tyweli.

CARMARTHEN TO ABERYSTWYTH

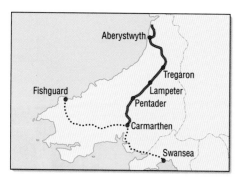

Two of the most important stations in west Wales in the heyday of the railway were Aberystwyth and Carmarthen. Today they are shadows of their former selves, Aberystwyth the end of a meandering branch from Dovey Junction, Carmarthen a terminus by default and an inconvenient reversal point for trains to Pembroke and Fishguard. It is still possible to travel by train between the two places but it would require an interminable and completely impractical journey via Shrewsbury, Craven Arms and Llanelli. Until the 1960s things were different, and it was possible to travel directly from Carmarthen to Aberystwyth, a 56-mile journey scheduled to take about 2 hours 30 minutes.

The story of this line goes back to 1854, and the setting up of the Carmarthen & Cardigan Railway. Constant financial problems limited progress and by 1864 it had only reached Pencader. Cardigan remained firmly out of reach. Eventually it was sorted out, largely by the GWR. The remains of the planned main line north of Pencader became the Newcastle Emlyn branch, opened in 1895, and a new main line was built up to Aberystwyth via Lampeter. Later came a branch to Aberaeron, opened by the Lampeter, Aberayron & New Quay Light Railway in 1911. Meanwhile, Cardigan did finally receive its own railway in 1886, but from a totally different direction, from Whitland, well to the west of Carmarthen. These railways served a predominantly rural and underpopulated region, with little

▼ As a major rail centre, Carmarthen had a large and well-equipped station capable of handling mainline expresses, local services and a wide range of goods traffic, as shown by this 1930s view. Today the station, much reduced, and is the end of the line, with buffers replacing the level crossing.

▲ Pencader, seen here in the 1950s still looking like a typical GWR country town station, was the junction for the Newcastle Emlyn branch. The nature of traffic on the line is shown by the oil tank wagon attached to the end of the passenger train.

wo of the most important stations in west
Wales in the heyday of the railway were
Aberystwyth and Carmarthen. Today they are
shadows of their former selves, Aberystwyth the
end of a meandering branch from Dovey Junction,
Carmarthen a terminus by default and an
inconvenient reversal point for trains to Pembroke
and Fishguard. It is still possible to travel by train
between the two places but it would require an
interminable and completely impractical journey
via Shrewsbury, Craven Arms and Llanelli. Until
the 1960s things were different, and it was
possible to travel directly from Carmarthen to
Aberystwyth, a 56-mile journey scheduled to take about 2 hours 30 minutes.

The story of this line goes back to 1854, and the setting up of the Carmarthen
& Cardigan Railway. Constant financial problems limited progress and by 1864
it had only reached Pencader. Cardigan remained firmly out of reach. Eventually
it was sorted out, largely by the GWR. The remains of the planned main line
north of Pencader became the Newcastle Emlyn branch, opened in 1895, and a
new main line was built up to Aberystwyth via Lampeter. Later came a branch to
Aberaeron, opened by the Lampeter, Aberayron & New Quay Light Railway in
1911. Meanwhile, Cardigan did finally receive its own railway in 1886, but from a

▲ This busy scene of horses being unloaded
on to a crowded platform for Lampeter Fair
in about 1912 shows how vital the railway
was in the life of small rural communities.

▼ Much of the route of the line can be
traced, and there are a number of tangible
reminders of its life, including this metal
bridge across the Teifi near Lampeter.

◄ Aberystwyth station was built by the Cambrian Railway in 1864, but much of what can be seen today reflects later work by the GWR, mostly in the 1920s.

► Llanrhystyd Road was the first station on the line south from Aberystwyth. In the 1950s, when this photograph was taken, there were only four trains a day each way to keep the stationmaster occupied.

▼ West of Llanilar, the route can be seen as a low embankment along the valley, marked by a line of trees. This is a familiar way of identifying a lost railway in the landscape.

MOAT LANE TO THREE COCKS

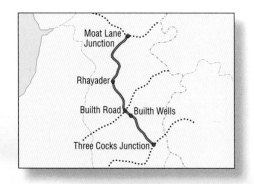

▼ A dramatic survivor is this cutting near the site of Glanyrafon Halt, seen from the adjacent overbridge. It shows the lasting impact on the landscape sometimes left by a long-closed railway.

The railway history of mid-Wales is curiously complicated. It starts in the region between Welshpool and Brecon in 1853, with the authorization of the Llanidloes & Newtown Railway. This short and completely isolated line opened six years later, and it was not until 1861 that it was joined to the outside world by the opening of the Oswestry & Newtown Railway. Other connections then came rapidly, the Newtown & Machynlleth westwards towards the coast and the Mid-Wales southwards from Llanidloes to Three Cocks Junction, where it met the line operated by the Hereford, Hay & Brecon Railway. By the mid-1860s all was in place. Some of these companies were then merged to form the Cambrian Railways, along with the Aberystwyth & Welsh Coast. However, the Mid-Wales managed to retain its independence until 1904. Tourist traffic helped to keep the lines running, and during World War I the route from Three Cocks Junction to Moat Lane Junction was used intensively by coal trains going from

▲ In June 1962 closure was a few months away, but this evocative picture shows that tourists were still using the line. A family with laden bicycles awaits the train, perhaps making the most of the local network before it disappeared. The station sign indicates the line's importance as a connecting route.

the South Wales coalfields to Scapa Flow. Also helpful was the connection near Builth Wells with the line from Shrewsbury to Swansea and Llanelli. Backed by the L&NWR, the latter had been completed in 1868 after an equally tortuous gestation period. Another major connecting line, the Manchester & Milford Haven, was planned in the 1860s but not completed, though a short section was built south of Llanidloes towards Llangurig but never opened. In fact, competition between the GWR and the L&NWR had inspired the building of much of this network and its legacy could still be seen even after the 1923 Grouping and into the era of British Railways.

Closures started quite early, with some minor parts of the network vanishing in the 1940s. Moat Lane Junction to Three Cocks Junction kept going for another two decades but the end, a pre-Beeching closure, came in December 1962. Despite this, there is still plenty to be seen, though not at either end. Moat Lane is a timber yard and Three Cocks an industrial site. The route follows three rivers, the Severn, the Dulas and the Wye, and can be traced in many places, for example as an embankment, or in a deep cutting near the site of Glanyrafon Halt. South of St Harmon, it joins the Wye valley, and from here more detailed exploration is worthwhile, with sections available as footpaths, notably Sustrans Route 8 and the Wye Valley Walk. Near Gilfach there is a tunnel and a well-preserved bridge. Rhayader station survives but is inaccessible and at Builth Road, still open on the Central Wales line, the site of the old lower station and yard can be seen. Erwood station has been restored as a café, with some track and old wagons, and a picnic site. Much of this section is on the Wye Valley Walk. There are some surprising survivals along the route, including bridges and platelayers' huts.

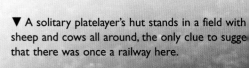

▼ A solitary platelayer's hut stands in a field with sheep and cows all around, the only clue to sugge that there was once a railway here.

RAILWAY STATION. NEWBRIDGE-ON-WYE.

◄ This Edwardian card of Newbridge-on-Wye station hints at a leisurely world, with plenty of time to pose for the photographer who stands, as so often, on the track.

◄ In the late 1950s a train pulls slowly into Rhayader, hauled by an ex-LMS Ivatt 2-6-0 locomotive. By then only three trains a day went all the way from Moat Lane Junction to Three Cocks Junction, leaving plenty of time for staff to tend the station garden.

► On a wet day in August 1962, it is unusually busy at Three Cocks Junction as three trains meet. The two on the left, from Brecon and Moat Lane Junction, are on the old Mid-Wales route via Builth, while the other has come from Hereford. Today nothing remains from this scene.

LOST STATIONS: WALES

A major legacy of the Victorian era in Wales was a fairly comprehensive railway network. The industrial areas of the south were served by an extraordinary density of lines linking the Valleys to Swansea and Cardiff. West of Carmarthen, ports, harbours and holiday traffic had put many places on the railway map, while another line went northwards to Aberystwyth and beyond, serving long branches along the route. To the east, other lines crossed the principality to connect with the network that followed the border. In the north-west, lines serving the slate trade and Snowdonia also linked Bangor with Pwllheli, making it possible to travel by train along much of the Welsh coastline. Even Anglesey had its own network. Until the 1960s, travelling around Wales by train was entirely practical, and often more efficient than by any other means. All this was soon to change as the closure programmes tore the network apart, leaving a hotchpotch of largely disconnected fragments. Two main lines, along the north and south coasts, remained, along with one across the centre of Wales to Aberystwyth. The route along the western coast was fragmented, and Carmarthen became a dead end. Border and Valley lines survived, but much reduced. The Heart of Wales line from Craven Arms to Llanelli was spared but all its branchline connections were severed, as were vital rail links between Bangor and Afonwen and south from Aberystwyth. Many towns and villages were plunged back into the isolation of the pre-railway age, a pattern of change made worse by the gradual collapse of the core industries and the steady decline of coal mining. Hundreds of stations were closed and many simply abandoned, subsequently to be demolished or turned into something else.

▼ The Bala & Dolgelly Railway, completed in 1870, was part of a route that crossed Wales from Barmouth to Ruabon, with important connections along the way. The line was closed in 1965. This shows the once-pretty station at Dolgellau, at the western end, some years later.

▲ In about 1900 Aberaman station, on the Taff Vale line from Abercynon to Aberdare, is being enlarged to cater for expanding traffic and to serve better the industries of the Valleys. Sixty years later many of these lines were being closed, and Aberaman is no more.

▲ In 1962 nature has taken over the former trackbed at Govilon station, on the Merthyr line west of Abergavenny. Closure had come four years earlier, but everything was still in good order, including the LNWR station nameboard.

▼ A fall of snow blankets Talyllyn Junction station and a train vanishes into its own smokescreen. It is 28 December 1962; just three days later the station, the Brecon line to Newport and its connecting network would be closed for ever.

LOST JOURNEY: AMLWCH TO LLANGOLLEN

The railway from Chester to Holyhead was one of Britain's first main lines, and this became a backbone for a network of lines spreading into the heart of North Wales. It also forms the major part of this journey, from Gaerwen to Rhyl. By the end of the Victorian period, Wales was well served by railways and most towns of any size were connected to the network. It was territory fought over by the GWR, the LNWR and the Midland, resulting in a number of lines across demanding country in order to serve small communities. This is a typical journey across the principality, probably taken for reasons of work or for a family visit. Considering the distance and the number of changes, it was relatively quick and straightforward, with only one poor connection at Corwen. It offered a changing vision of the Welsh landscape, from rugged Anglesey and the Menai Straits to the northern coastline and then south through softer country to the valley of the Dee. Today, though sections of the route survive, both as part of the national network and as a preserved railway, it is an impossible journey by train.

TIMETABLE	
Amlwch.....................	8.15am
Gaerwen...................	8.58am
Change	
Gaerwen...................	9.07am
Rhyl..........................	10.37am
Change	
Rhyl..........................	11.05am
Denbigh....................	11.35am
Change	
Denbigh....................	12.05pm
Corwen.....................	12.54pm
Change	
Corwen.....................	2.40pm
Llangollen................	3.20pm

AMLWCH

Conway

Britannia Bridge

Bangor

GAERWEN

▶ THE LONG BRANCH across Anglesey to Amlwch was completed in 1867 and continued to carry passengers for nearly a century, until 1964. The station was a decorative building, overpowered by the large goods shed. There was a good service, with up to ten trains a day.

◀ THE HIGHLIGHT of the journey, and one of Britain's greatest engineering feats of the Victorian age, was Robert Stephenson's Britannia bridge. Completed in 1850, it was formed of two iron box tubes through which the trains ran. As such, it was a larger version of the bridge already built by Stephenson at Conway. Each end was guarded by massive stone lions, carved by John Thomas; their power and scale are apparent in this Edwardian postcard. The bridge was rebuilt in the 1970s after a disastrous fire.

Miniature Train, Marine Lake, Rhyl

◀ RHYL WAS A RESORT before the railway came, but its growth was largely in the late-Victorian era, when much of Wales's northern coast was developed. It was a town of hotels and seaside pleasures and had a famous miniature railway. Sadly, with only 30 minutes between trains on this journey, there was no time to visit the railway, beach or town.

▼ ALL THE SECTIONS of this journey were built separately, mostly by small companies. The Llangollen & Corwen opened its stretch of line along the Dee valley in 1865. Corwen, as this 1906 card indicates, is pleasantly sited south of the river. The railway embankment can be seen beside the Dee; the station is off to the left. With a long wait, there would be time to explore Corwen's associations with the Welsh nationalist leader Owain Glyndwr.

RHYL

DENBIGH

Ruthin

CORWEN   LLANGOLLEN

Corwen.

B. 39398. LLANGOLLEN: FROM THE BRIDGE.

▶ LLANGOLLEN'S STATION sits right beside the fast-flowing river Dee, as this 1912 card shows. The line from Corwen was closed in 1964 but most of it has since been reopened as a preserved steam railway, so the final section of this journey, a pretty run beside the river, can now be enjoyed again.

EXCURSION TRAINS

From the 1840s until the last years of British Rail, excursions formed a significant part of regular railway business. Over many decades individual companies, and then the various regions of the nationalized network, competed fiercely in the pursuit of custom. Most excursions were simply to resorts or places of interest, but many were more adventurous, combining train travel with coach tours or river and sea trips. Those with special interests, such as walkers, sports enthusiasts, nature lovers, photographers or shoppers, were also catered for. Some excursions were timed to coincide with regular holiday periods, such as Wakes Weeks, while others tried to make the most of off-peak travel. There were also private excursions, run specially for groups or by companies for their employees. Also important throughout much of the 20th century were excursions run by or for rail enthusiasts, often featuring rare or unusual locomotives and vehicles or visiting remote parts of the network and lines threatened with closure.

For Stay-at-Home Holidaymakers

DURING THE WEEKS COMMENCING
4th, 11th, 18th and 25th JULY, 22nd and 29th AUGUST and 5th SEPTEMBER, 1960

SPECIAL
HOLIDAY RUNABOUT RAIL TICKET
FOR
COAST and COUNTRY

BRITISH RAILWAYS

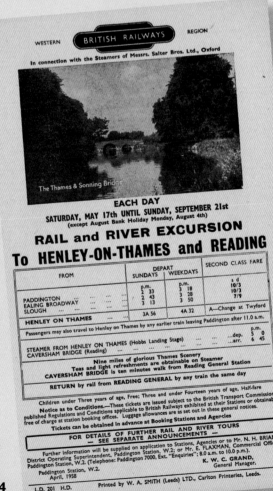

BRITISH RAILWAYS

WESTERN   REGION

In connection with the Steamers of Messrs. Salter Bros. Ltd., Oxford

The Thames & Sonning Bridge

EACH DAY
SATURDAY, MAY 17th UNTIL SUNDAY, SEPTEMBER 21st
(except August Bank Holiday Monday, August 4th)

RAIL and RIVER EXCURSION
To HENLEY-ON-THAMES and READING

FROM	DEPART SUNDAYS	DEPART WEEKDAYS	SECOND CLASS FARE
	p.m.	p.m.	s d
PADDINGTON	2 33	3 18	10/3
EALING BROADWAY	2 43	3 28	10/3
SLOUGH	3 13	3 50	7/9
HENLEY ON THAMES	3A 56	4A 32	A—Change at Twyford

Passengers may also travel to Henley on Thames by any earlier train leaving Paddington after 11.0 a.m.

STEAMER FROM HENLEY ON THAMES (Hobbs Landing Stage)		...dep.	5 0
CAVERSHAM BRIDGE (Reading)		...arr.	6 45

Nine miles of glorious Thames Scenery
Teas and light refreshments are obtainable on Steamer
CAVERSHAM BRIDGE is ten minutes walk from Reading General Station

RETURN by rail from READING GENERAL by any train the same day

Children under Three years of age, Free; Three and under Fourteen years of age, Half-fare
Notice as to Conditions.—These tickets are issued subject to the British Transport Commission's published Regulations and Conditions applicable to British Railways exhibited at their Stations or obtainable free of charge at station booking offices. Luggage allowances are as set out in these general notices.

Tickets can be obtained in advance at Booking Stations and Agencies

FOR DETAILS OF FURTHER RAIL AND RIVER TOURS —
SEE SEPARATE ANNOUNCEMENTS —

Further information will be supplied on application to Stations, Agencies or to Mr. N. H. BRIANT, District Operating Superintendent, Paddington Station, W.2; or Mr. E. FLAXMAN, Commercial Officer, Paddington Station, W.2 (Telephone: Paddington 7000, Ext. "Enquiries"; 8.0 a.m. to 10.0 p.m.).
K. W. C. GRAND,
April, 1958   General Manager.

L.D. 201 H.D.   Printed by W. A. SMITH (Leeds) LTD., Carlton Printeries, Leeds.

▲ This 1960 handbill was designed to attract the 'Stay-at-Home Holidaymakers', those who wanted to do their own thing during the official Edinburgh and Glasgow Trades Holiday period, from July to early September.

◄ The combined rail and river trip was perennially popular, as underlined by this 1958 handbill. In this case, daily summer services were offered from London to Reading or Henley, with 'nine miles of glorious Thames Scenery'.

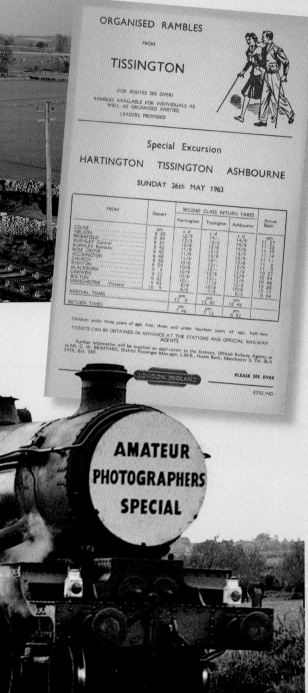

▲ The Cromford & High Peak Railway in Derbyshire, which closed in the 1960s, was primarily a freight line whose route featured fearsome inclines. Shortly before closure, these attracted many enthusiasts' specials.

▼ Special interest groups were well catered for. Here, in 1958, an amateur photographers' special, organized in conjunction with the GWR, passes Pebworth Halt, probably on its way to or from Stratford-on-Avon.

◄ In the 1960s the steam age was rapidly drawing to a close, so the number of steam specials greatly increased. Favoured particularly were famous classes of locomotives, such as the LNER Gresley A4s. In September 1966, no. 60019, 'Bittern', hauled the last A4 excursion to Aberdeen.

▼ Corporate excursions were an important part of railway business. Here, a special organized in the 1950s by the Northern Rubber Company, featuring veteran Great Central Railway 440 no. 62666 'Zeebrugge' and former LNER teak carriages, approaches High Wycombe.

◄ In Scotland rail and steamer tours were always popular. This 1966 handbill offers adventurous tours, on summer Tuesdays, Thursdays and Saturdays, of lochs Long, Goil and Lomond, with travel by train, steamer and coach.

Popular and interesting

DAY CIRCULAR TOUR No. 5

to the

3 - LOCHS

LOCH LONG, LOCH GOIL
AND LOCH LOMOND

BY TRAIN AND STEAMER

Season 1966

▶ Famous Victorian and Edwardian locomotives were often used to haul specials in the British Railways era. The last Great Northern Ivatt Atlantic in service, no. 62822, built in 1902, made its final run on 26 November 1950, from Kings Cross to Doncaster.

GOODS WAGONS

One of the great pleasures of trainspotting in the steam age was noting the extraordinary variety of goods wagons to be seen in mixed-freight trains. In the early days, freight was often more important than passengers, with specialized vehicles dedicated to the safe carriage of particular products and materials. Each railway company had its own fleet of goods vehicles and the specialized designs were fairly universal. As many wagons looked similar, their purpose was clearly labelled on the outside. From the start, wagons were built from wood, with a metal chassis or frame, and the vast majority had four wheels, simple buffers and couplings, and minimal brakes – a pattern that remained largely unchanged until the second half of the 20th century. In fact the survival of huge varieties of small vehicles with limited carrying capacity greatly hindered the development of modern freight-handling systems. When British Railways was formed, it inherited over a million goods wagons, with more than 400 different types represented. Many lingered on in remote sidings well into the 1980s.

▲ A typical late-Victorian wooden-bodied wagon with metal frames and pitched roof, built for the carriage of Manger's salt.

► There were many kinds of tank wagon. This is a Somerset & Dorset version, designed for the storage of gas.

▲ Fruit required special handling and often travelled in vans built for faster running. This is a GNR banana van.

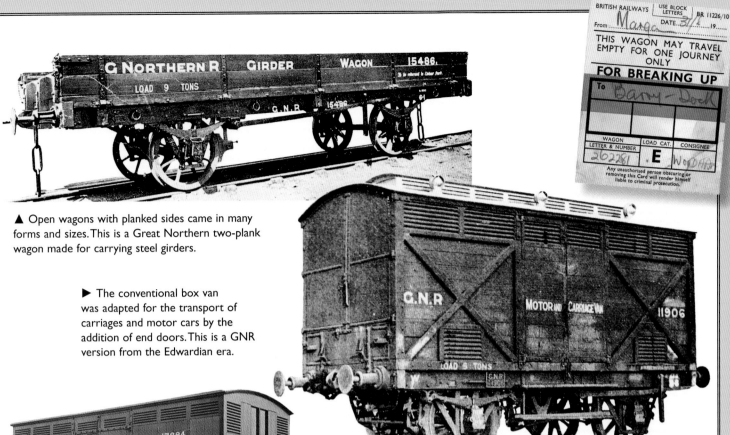

G NORTHERN R GIRDER WAGON 15486
LOAD 9 TONS
G.N.R 15486

▲ Open wagons with planked sides came in many forms and sizes. This is a Great Northern two-plank wagon made for carrying steel girders.

▶ The conventional box van was adapted for the transport of carriages and motor cars by the addition of end doors. This is a GNR version from the Edwardian era.

G.N.R MOTOR AND CARRIAGE VAN 11906
LOAD 5 TONS
G.N.R 11906

M CALF VAN R 17884
TO BE RETURNED TO DERBY CATTLE DOCKS WHEN EMPTY
MIDLAND 17884

◀ Livestock transport was a major business and most railways had specialized cattle wagons. This is a Midland calf van, built in Derby in 1908.

▼ Freight carriage rates were determined by weight, so weighing machinery had to be regularly checked for accuracy, often by special vehicles such as this Midland example.

GUNPOWDER VAN
N
20457

◀ There were many dangerous cargoes, notably chemicals, petrol, oil and gunpowder, that required special vehicles. Gunpowder vans, such as this GNR example, were usually painted red.

WEIGHING MACHINE ADJUSTING VAN.
NOT TO BE DELAYED IN TRANSIT.
MIDLAND 18
6·4·3

▼ Specialized wagons were used until the 1960s and beyond, as indicated by this *Know Your Trains* educational folder, published by the British Transport Commission in about 1960. It identified most current wagons.

CARE & REPAIR

Steam locomotives were demanding machines, requiring constant attention. Apart from regular coaling, watering and ash removal, there was a continual round of oiling, greasing and adjustment to be carried out on shed, in the sidings or yards or at station stops. Quality of performance was related directly to maintenance, so both driver and fireman were always busy. Their jobs required a unique combination of experience, instinct, anticipation and dedication, but for all that it was a highly regulated industry, with rules and rule books to cover most eventualities. Driver and fireman were in charge of their locomotive while it was in their care but the more major maintenance work was carried out by the engineers attached to the sheds. This could range from day-to-day maintenance to major repairs and overhauls. While coaling and ash removal were usually shed activities, water was a constant requirement, so water columns and towers were universal in the steam age, and every station of any stature would have at least one. Rolling stock, signalling equipment and the track itself were also subject to scheduled maintenance programmes.

THE BRITISH TRANSPORT COMMISSION
BRITISH RAILWAYS

REGULATIONS

FOR THE GUIDANCE
OF

TRAIN EXAMINERS
GREASERS AND OILERS

OCTOBER 1953

▲ In the railway world there were rules and regulations about everything, and the smooth operation of the network was entirely dependent upon their being strictly adhered to.

▼ An old Drummond 0-6-0 Jumbo takes on water at Motherwell in the 1950s while the crew enjoy a short breather. With care and good maintenance, an ancient locomotive could work for decades.

◄ LNER class B1 'Topi' receives some minor attention at the end of the Meltham branch, near the junction with the Huddersfield-to-Penistone line, which lies beyond the signal box.

► A serious discussion, apparently about oiling, takes place between the driver and fireman of class A1 locomotive 60143 'Sir Walter Scott' at Newcastle shed while the wheel-tapper looks on.

◀▲ Aspects of locomotive maintenance, on shed and on the road, are captured in photographs taken at Newcastle in the 1950s. These range from setting the head code (top left) to cleaning out the tubes, always a thankless and unpopular job (bottom left).

▼ Water towers, of constantly varied form, were positioned at regular intervals throughout the network. Here, in June 1960, GWR Prairie tank no. 4557 takes water at Glogue Halt, while the passengers in the 4.00pm Whitland-to-Cardigan train enjoy the sunshine through the windows.

▶ Locomotives on branchline duties might be away from the main shed for days on end, so regular maintenance was down to the crew. This was usually carried out at the line's terminus, where limited facilities were available. At Lyme Regis in Dorset, in August 1945, the fireman from Adams radial tank no. 520 gets down to the task of removing cinders from the smokebox.

◀ Track maintenance was also demanding. Here, at Eridge, near Tunbridge Wells, in 1932, water is taken into the old tenders used for weed killing along the line, while interested spectators look on.

▼ A smart Stanier Black Five stands by the coaling tower at Kentish Town shed, in north London, on a sunny day in 1958, while an equally smart, and very lucky, trainspotter has made sure that his friend records the moment.

VIADUCTS

When lines were closed, much of their infrastructure was removed within a short period of time. Buildings, however, tended to remain in situ. Former stations and goods sheds can still be seen all over Britain, but it is the thousands of surviving bridges and viaducts that are the enduring legacy of the railway age. Viaducts, in stone, brick, iron or concrete, striding across valleys and rivers, retain their grandeur and excitement long after the trains have ceased to run over them. Many have been demolished, including some of the greatest, but there are spectacular survivors. Some are now privately owned, some are the lasting responsibility of Network Rail, and a number have been protected by the listing process. Many are inaccessible, while others carry footpaths and cycletracks. Old viaducts offer more than just memories of railways long gone: in so many places, they continue to make a major contribution to their surrounding landscape, whether it be rural or urban. They are also memorials to Victorian engineering.

▼ The Crumlin viaduct was, at nearly 200ft, the highest in Britain when completed in 1857 by the Newport, Abergavenny & Hereford Railway. This 1963 photograph shows the remarkable nature of its scale and the iron trestle construction. It was demolished in 1965.

▲ When it opened in 1878, the Tay bridge was the longest in Britain and one of the wonders of the world. On 28 December 1879 it collapsed in a storm, taking with it a train and seventy-eight people. This bizarre memorial card shows all the tickets collected from the passengers before the train crossed.

▲ In 1879 a railway bridge was opened across the Severn. Later the new tunnel took much of the traffic but the bridge remained in use until October 1960, when a barge demolished two of the twenty-one spans.

◄ A notably elegant viaduct was built in 1858 across Hownes Gill, near Consett, by the Stockton & Darlington Railway. It now carries a footpath.

▼ In 1965 three lines served Whitby, from north, south and west. Here, a train from Scarborough crosses the magnificent Larpool viaduct on its way to Whitby West Cliff, with two other lines beneath the viaduct. Now, only the line along the river bank to Middlesbrough survives, but the viaduct still stands.

BESIDE THE TRACK

Something that used to enliven the journeys of keen-eyed passengers is the amazing number and variety of signs and bits of equipment there used to be alongside the line. Most obvious were the signals and the signalling infrastructure, along with the machinery that made the railways operate properly and safely, such as point levers. However, there was very much more than this, all of it integral to the railway scene across the network but now lost for ever. The list included mileposts, gradient posts, bridge plates and boundary markers, all of which reflected the concern for precision, detail and order that characterized the railway age. Equally impressive was the variety of signs. Made of wood, concrete, cast iron and enamel, most were warnings or admonitions, often written in forms of English that now seem archaic and pedantic. In the Victorian and Edwardian eras, each railway company had its own style and colours, adding greatly to the diversity of these signs; many were still in use decades after the formation of the Big Four in 1923. Aside from signs, there were also the more significant lineside structures: the platelayers' huts, the water towers, the loading gauges, the water troughs between the tracks. Then there were the thousands of miles of telegraph and telephone wires looping along between the wooden posts that lined even the most minor railway; each wire was connected to a ceramic insulator, which was frequently stamped with the initials of the railway company that owned the line. The corporate image, or house style, was of great importance, and often a matter of pride, to the railway companies, and trackside equipment was just as vital a component of that image as the stations and the trains. Even the most minor things carried the company name or monogram and those that survive naturally appeal to both the historian and the collector.

▼ Most signs were factory-made to well-defined styles and specifications, but the trackside was also littered with 'home-made' examples, often produced in local workshops. Many were delightfully eccentric, like this one near Liskeard, Cornwall.

ONLY UNCOLOURED
06 0T YELLOW 45XX AND
57XX 97XX ENGINES MAY
PASS THIS BOARD

▲ A Victorian concern for detail ensured that railway companies marked the limits of their territory. Fencing was the most common marker, but also used were cast-iron boundary posts bearing the company's initials, in this case those of the Mid Wales Railway.

▲ Steam locomotives need constant supplies of water. In the 1860s an automatic means of refilling the tender was developed, whereby a scoop lowered by the fireman collected water from long troughs laid between the tracks. Here, a Britannia class 4-6-2, no. 70021 'Morning Star', passes over Bushey troughs, in Hertfordshire, with a fitted freight.

4-6-0 No. 1023 'County of Oxford' County Class. Great Western Railway. *Driving wheels 6' 3". Two cylinders 18½" diam. x 30"* *stroke. Boiler pressure 250 lb/in². Tractive effort 29,050 lb.*

▲ Lineside mileposts, marking each quarter, half and full mile, were a feature of early railways and were made compulsory by an Act of 1845. Made in wood, iron and, later, concrete, these varied in style – as indicated on this 1930s GWR postcard.

▶ In the past even the smallest station had sidings, and the sets of points that accessed these were controlled by hand-operated levers of the kind shown here. Some survive around the network but are relatively rare.

▼ Changes in ownership often gave rise to groups of lineside signs, especially of the type giving warnings to the public. Here, near Betchworth, Surrey, there were two signs in cast iron, from L&SWR and SE&CR, a battered enamel one from the Southern and a delightfully worded but clearly handmade wooden one from British Railways.

▲ The platelayers' hut was a common lineside feature and quite a number have lived on long after closure of the line they served. This one is on the M&GN network in Norfolk.

◄ Old iron signs littered the network until the 1980s, but survivors in situ are now rare. This example is in a hedge near Wisbech.

▲ Cast-iron boundary markers, generally being small and unobtrusive, often get overlooked and left behind by the salvage gangs following line closures. This example survives at Lartington, near Barnard Castle.

▲ All railway companies were concerned about trespassers, so notices threatening prosecution were put up with great frequency. Usually made in cast iron, these varied widely in style, size and message from company to company. Such notices are not uncommon today but their appeal to the collector is dependent upon their rarity. A dual-language one like this, issued by a minor company, the Brecon & Merthyr Railway, would be far more appealing than a standard GWR example.

◄ Station nameboards came in many shapes and styles, in wood, metal, enamel, concrete and even plastic. Legibility was the aim, and some companies favoured raised lettering, believing the shadow would make it show up better. Great care was taken with punctuation.

► A delightful and common statement of individuality was the marking of station names in unusual ways. White-painted stones, set into gravel or grass, were popular, but grand stations justified grander schemes, as in this fine example from York.

▼ Maker's plates were to be found on many things, from locomotives and wagons to station girders, signal posts and bridges. This example is on a bridge near Masbury, on the former Somerset & Dorset line.

► Some trespass notices can be dated by the names included in the message, such as this NER example, now preserved and attached to the wall of a former station in the Whitby area, North Yorkshire.

▼ The comprehension of important information was often hindered by a complex and archaic use of English. British Railways seemed to make a point of this, as this crossing warning sign demonstrates.

NORTH EASTERN RAILWAY
PUBLIC WARNING
PERSONS ARE WARNED NOT TO TRESPASS ON THIS RAILWAY, OR ON ANY OF THE LINES, STATIONS, WORKS, OR PREMISES CONNECTED THEREWITH.
ANY PERSON SO TRESPASSING IS LIABLE TO A PENALTY OF FORTY SHILLINGS.
C. N. WILKINSON
SECRETARY.

B.R. NOTICE
PASSENGERS ARE REQUESTED NOT TO CROSS THE LINE, UNTIL THE TRAIN HAS DEPARTED SO THEY MAY AVOID DANGER IN CASE TRAIN MAY BE APPROACHING ON THE OPPOSITE SIDE.   BY ORDER.

... AND EVEN MORE LOST LIVERIES

◄ One of the stranger liveries created by British Rail during its latter years was this one for Rail Express Systems, used largely for parcels and mail traffic. 47727 'Duke of Edinburgh's Award' shows that this livery always looked like an unfinished paint job.

▼ Speedlink was formed in 1977 and by the late 1980s a two-tone grey livery was in use, adorned with colourful symbols depicting various areas of bulk cargo activity, such as steel, coal or stone. Speedlink vanished in July 1991, turning briefly into Transrail, before all freight traffic went into the private sector.

◄ Network SouthEast, with its distinctive livery and branding, was formed in the 1980s to operate through much of southern England.

▼ A class 20 diesel stands at Bescot, Walsall, in 1992, displaying the grey version of the BR big symbol livery.

◀ InterCity was one of the sectors of railway activity that emerged from the restructuring of 1982. From this time, British Rail's mainline passenger services were very business-orientated and were marked by a smart livery that was applied to both the locomotives and the carriages.

▶ There were many variants of British Rail's blue livery, with numerous changes to the size and placing of the locomotive's number and the BR symbol. This particular version was photographed in 1989 at Oxford on 50031 'Hood'.

▼ By the late 1980s British Rail had overcome its aversion to history, and locomotives began to appear with historical paint finishes. Here, in 1993, a class 40 diesel has been outshopped as D306, in the colours of the late 1950s and early 1960s.

▲ In 1976 British Rail introduced the first of a large fleet of HST 125s, sets of six or eight carriages with a diesel-electric power car at each end, designed for sustained speeds of 125mph. They had for a while the striking blue-and-yellow livery shown on this detail from a promotional leaflet.

CENTRAL
ENGLAND

LOST & FOUND

THERE IS SOMETHING ROMANTIC about overgrown and abandoned railway track. This is Cauldon, the end of the old mineral line from Stoke-on-Trent.

LOST & FOUND: CENTRAL ENGLAND

▼ A CRUMBLING BRIDGE lost in the landscape is often a lasting memorial to a long-dead line. This fine example in engineering brick marks the route of the former Tetbury branch in Gloucestershire, closed in 1964.

▲ A SPLENDID ITALIANATE VILLA of a station, built for the Earl of Shrewsbury in 1849, Alton Towers still surveys the route of the North Staffordshire Railway's rural Churnet Valley line.

ROSS-ON-WYE TO CHEPSTOW

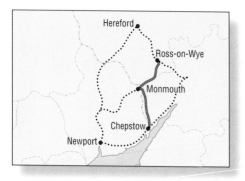

There was an extensive network of railways between Hereford and the river Severn but nothing remains today except the line from Gloucester to Newport, along the river's western shore. Preservationists are active in the Forest of Dean and around Lydney but far too much has been lost, including one of the most scenic railway journeys in Britain, the route along the Wye valley. The first railway to Ross-on-Wye was the line from Hereford to Gloucester, opened in 1855. Monmouth was put on the map two years later, with the completion of the line from Pontypool and Usk and on towards Coleford. It was now logical to link the two towns and this was done by the Ross & Monmouth Railway in 1873, with a later connection to the Pontypool line at Monmouth Troy station. Freight was the driving force behind much of this development, including the last link in the chain, a connecting line south along the Wye valley from Monmouth to Chepstow. This, a notably picturesque route following the bends of the river, criss-crossing the border between England and Wales and passing close to Tintern Abbey, was completed by

▲ This early view of Lydbrook shows the railway viaduct that took the railway high above the town. At Lydbrook Junction there was a connecting line to the Forest of Dean network and on to Parkend and Lydney.

201 c. Symonds Yat Station.

◀ Symonds Yat was the most scenic spot on the Wye between Ross and Monmouth and it had a suitably picturesque station with plenty of cottagey details, clearly apparent in this Edwardian postcard.

▼ There are no railways in Monmouth today but the town has plenty of reminders of its railway past. Set in the steep-sided Wye valley, the town demanded extravagant railway structures. These two viaducts reflect that: the girder bridge brought the Ross line into Monmouth, while the stone one carried the Chepstow line.

the nominally independent Wye Valley Railway in 1876. Soon, it was all under the control of the GWR, by which time tourist traffic along the Wye valley was developing. For this reason, closure to passengers, when it came in 1959, was rather a surprise. Freight traffic lingered on for a few years.

Fifty or so years later, much of the route survives and it can easily be explored via the official Wye Valley Walk. This allows walkers to enjoy the same views that made the line so appealing to train passengers, including the splendid sight of the ruins of Tintern Abbey, the delights of Symonds Yat and the now fully restored Tintern station.

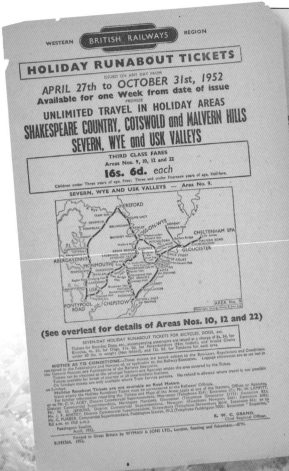

▲ ◀ Monmouth had two stations, May Hill and Troy, and the latter, seen here in the 1950s, was the one for the Wye valley line. The tourist potential of the line was well understood, and it was widely promoted. This Holiday Runabout leaflet, issued by British Railways in 1952, includes the whole route, along with other lines in the area.

◄ Tintern station, now a listed building and a famous feature on the Wye Valley Walk, is a kind of time warp, preserved for ever in some undefined GWR golden age. Luggage waits on the platform and there is a café and a museum. The only things missing are the track and the trains.

▼ On its route along the Wye valley, the railway went over the river several times, simultaneously criss-crossing the border between Wales and England. At Redbrook, to the south of Monmouth, a typical late-Victorian iron trestle bridge survives, high above the river and its densely wooded banks.

CHELTENHAM TO KING'S SUTTON

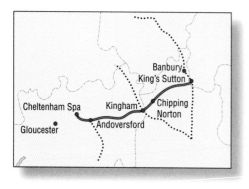

The railway from Cheltenham to King's Sutton was a meandering route, mostly through the attractive landscape of the Cotswolds. It was always a typical rural railway and by the late 1940s there was only one through train a day, which took three hours to cover the 44 miles, allowing plenty of time to enjoy the scenery. As with so many minor lines, the history was complicated. It started in the 1850s with the Chipping Norton Railway, a short line connecting the town with the main Oxford-to-Worcester line at Kingham (then known as Chipping Norton Junction). By 1862 passenger services had ceased. Next came the Bourton-on-the-Water Railway, whose short line westwards from Kingham opened in 1862. Plans to carry on to Cheltenham got nowhere. Nothing then happened until the 1880s, when another company, the Banbury & Cheltenham Direct, completed the missing sections from Bourton to Cheltenham and from Chipping Norton to King's Sutton on the Oxford-to-Banbury line. By 1897 it was absorbed into the GWR. The landscape made its own demands, with plenty of cuttings and embankments, a tunnel and a dramatic viaduct near Hook Norton. Never busy, the line was destined to close at some point and this process started in 1951, with the Chipping Norton to King's Sutton section. The rest followed eleven years later.

Today, the remains of the line reflect the different closure periods. West of Kingham, many of the distinctive engineering-brick bridges survive, while on the eastern section most of the

▲ Unexpected things can still be seen on long-lost railways, such as this battered but still identifiable concrete gradient post, east of Stow-on-the-Wold.

▼ This view of Notgrove was taken shortly before the line's closure in 1962. The train drifts into a deserted station on a summer's day, and the photographer's shadow is the only sign of life on the platform. There is not much to see today, as nature has reclaimed the site.

▲ A farm track through green fields west of Kingham still bears the unmistakable stamp of a lost railway.

▶ Kingham, known as Chipping Norton Junction until 1909, was a busy place. The lines towards King's Sutton branch away on the right; in the distance, over the passenger's head, is the bridge carrying the Cheltenham line. Today, the station is still open on the Oxford-to-Worcester line, but the bridge, signal box and all other structures are gone.

bridges have gone. Starting from Cheltenham, there is not much to be seen before Andoversford but eastwards from here the line can be traced through the hills and valleys in cuttings and embankments, clearly visible but largely inaccessible. Near Bourton the line follows the valley of the Windrush, and in Bourton the station unexpectedly survives, locked in a council yard. Kingham, now a simple station with an old GWR nameboard, was much more significant and the site of the former junction can be explored on footpaths. An industrial park has taken over much of the route around Chipping Norton but to the east the sites of remote halts can be traced. The approach to Hook Norton is now a nature reserve, with footpath access. In Bloxham the station site is largely built over but, incongruously, a footbridge survives, though inaccessible. Adderbury station is also an industrial site, even though this section remained open for goods for a few years. At King's Sutton modern trains roar through, but the old bay platform can still be identified, along with the site of the old junction.

▲ Bloxham station has gone and much of its site is now covered in houses. A metal footbridge survives, crossing the overgrown bit that remains, but seems to lead nowhere.

▲ The most accessible part of the route today is the area around Hook Norton tunnel, which is a nature reserve and footpath. The tunnel itself is bricked up but this bridge survives to the north of it.

▼ In landscape terms, the Hook Norton area is the most dramatic. The steep hills and valleys demanded deep cuttings, a tunnel and a high viaduct, whose tall stone piers still dominate the valley. This picture of Hook Norton station, with its steep approach, indicates the nature of the landscape. It is a complete railway scene, but nothing remains today.

► Rollright Halt was one of a number of minor stations along the line. This early picture shows the typical GWR pagoda-style shelter used in such locations. Today the embankment is overgrown and inaccessible and the bridge over the lane has gone, but the house is still there.

◄ Adderbury station is abandoned and the weeds are growing over the track in this 1960s photograph, taken after closure. None of the buildings shown here survive.

▼ King's Sutton is, remarkably, still alive, though most trains, like this Birmingham-bound Virgin Voyager, just race through. The remains of another platform can be seen on the left, while in the distance beyond the bridge a line of trees on the right marks the site of the junction with the Cheltenham line.

LOST STATIONS: CENTRAL ENGLAND

The Midlands always represented the heart of the English railway network, thanks to the many main lines that passed through the region, with important connections to most Midlands towns and cities. Railway building started early in central England, and much of the network was in place or under construction by the 1850s. This was also the heart of the railway industry, home to some of the most important company workshops, for example at Crewe and Derby. Goods traffic, both long-distance and local, was always important, notably coal and stone; this was the major source of wealth for the principal railway in the region, the famous Midland. However, there were many other railways, great and small, competing for the traffic and serving the more rural areas. The GWR fought to gain a foothold and then held on to its share, even into the days of British Railways. Inevitably, the region was densely packed with stations, particularly around the cities, and even in the country there were few places of any significance without access to the network. There was also much duplication of routes, so the impact of closure programmes was never as apparent as in country areas. Many stations did go but they were often on lines kept open for goods traffic. However, there were major losses, notably most of the Great Central's route and some lines through the spectacular scenery of Derbyshire. Also hit hard were the lines that crossed the region from west to east, connecting the main trunk routes.

▼ Railway rivalry gave Stroud two stations. One, on the old GWR main line from Swindon to Gloucester, is still in use. The other was at the end of a short branch from the Midland Railway's Stonehouse-to-Nailsworth branch line, itself linked to the MR's main line from Bristol to Gloucester. This MR Stroud branch was an early closure, to passengers in 1949. Goods traffic lingered on until 1 June 1966, shortly before this photograph was taken.

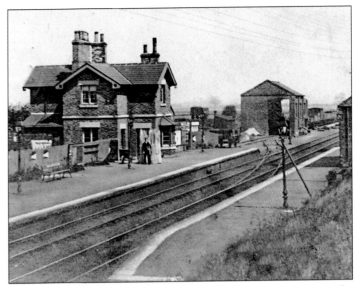

◀ Birmingham Snow Hill was built by the Great Western in 1912 as a reflection of its importance in the Midlands. Spacious, light and airy, it was seen in many ways as the perfect big city station. Closed in 1972, it was subsequently demolished, and then in 1987 a new Snow Hill was built to ease pressure on New Street.

▲ In this old view of Sturton station, on the former Great Central line from Retford to Gainsborough in Nottinghamshire, a porter poses by a stack of parcels on the otherwise deserted platform. Sturton closed in 1959, though the line is still open.

▼ Barnack, seen here in a derelict state long after the closure of the line from Wansford to Stamford in 1929, was in the heart of the Northamptonshire stone region. Many of the lines in this area were built specifically to serve the quarries, some of which had been in production since the Middle Ages.

LOST JOURNEY: CHELTENHAM TO PETERBOROUGH

The centre of England was blessed with a dense railway network, thanks partly to fierce competition during the early Victorian period and partly to the relatively easy nature of the landscape. As ever, the main routes ran south to north but in between was a mass of interconnecting lines. Journeys across the country were, therefore, quite easy, though sometimes slow and involving several changes. This is a journey entirely on these connecting lines, wandering across the country on trains from different companies, from one provincial town to another, from Gloucestershire to Cambridgeshire, and via some busy rail centres on main south-to-north lines. Such a journey might have been undertaken for business purposes, perhaps by a travelling salesman with his case of samples, the kind of professional person who was dependent on the railway system in its heyday. The 1960s cuts decimated these cross-country lines throughout the heart of England, removing at a stroke journeys of this type. Today the only way by train from Cheltenham to Peterborough is via Birmingham, but fragments of the original journey do still exist, including two short sections reopened as preserved lines.

TIMETABLE	
Cheltenham Malvern Rd	7.38am
Honeybourne......................	8.32am
Change	
Honeybourne......................	8.46am
Stratford-on-Avon...............	9.10am
Change	
Stratford-on-Avon...............	9.35am
Leamington Spa.................	10.12am
Change	
Leamington Spa.................	10.30am
Rugby...............................	11.05am
Change	
Rugby...............................	12.26pm
Peterborough.......................	11.05am

▲ THERE WERE SEVERAL STATIONS that included the word Cheltenham in their title, a reflection of the town's one-time importance as a rail centre. Most closed between 1962 and 1968, but one, Cheltenham Racecourse, has been reopened by a preserved railway. The photograph here shows Cheltenham Malvern Road, the starting point for this journey.

LEAMINGTON SPA

STRATFORD-ON-AVON

HONEYBOURNE

CHELTENHAM

▲ ON THIS JOURNEY there was no time to visit the Memorial Theatre in Stratford, but this card shows the view of the town and the Avon from the theatre's tower.

LEAMINGTON.
GREAT WESTERN RAILWAY.

◀ THIS GENERAL VIEW OF LEAMINGTON was issued by the GWR, perhaps to mark their railway dominance of the town. Posted in 1908, the postcard carries a message unrelated to this area: 'A passage cattle truck will be at Thatcham Wed morning by 8 o'clock. Put cattle on board by about 12 o'clock train & send to Twyford station.'

RUGBY

▶ THIS EDWARDIAN postcard of Rugby station, issued by the LNWR, shows that it was a busy place in that period. It was the meeting point for five lines, radiating in all directions, so there would be plenty of activity to watch during the wait of more than an hour on this journey, as well as kiosks and refreshment rooms to patronize.

CLOAK ROOM — WAY OUT — BOOKING OFFICE & GENERAL WAITING ROOM — TELEGRAPH OFFICE — TIME TABLES — PHŒNIX FIRE OFFICE — STEAM RAILWAY

LONDON & NORTH WESTERN RAILWAY COMPANY

BIRMINGHAM EXPRESS AT RUGBY PLATFORM.

CATHEDRAL FROM PALACE GARDENS

BRIDGE STREET

PETERBOROUGH CATHEDRAL FROM N.W.

PETERBOROUGH

CATHEDRAL FROM RIVER

THE PARK   L.1825

◀ PETERBOROUGH WAS another place that until the 1960s had several stations. This section of the journey, via Market Harborough, ended at Peterborough East, not the best for the city centre, but close enough for relatively easy access. The last few miles along the Nene valley have been reopened by a preserved railway.

CAR TRAINS

▲ One of a series of promotional postcards issued by British Rail's Motorail network in the 1970s, this shows a summer scene on a West Country service, with the typical flat trucks then in use.

On the first railways, horse-drawn carriages were transported on flat trucks, and later in covered wagons. This continued until the Edwardian era, when motor cars were first carried, notably by the Midland Railway from 1904. The Great Western also carried cars from 1909, on special services through the Severn Tunnel. However, it was not until the 1930s that the network saw regular long-distance services that carried both cars and passengers, notably between London and Scotland. Services were greatly expanded from the 1950s and by the 1960s the scheduled routes included London to several Scottish destinations, London to Cornwall, London to Fishguard, Newcastle to the West Country, the Midlands to Scotland, York to Inverness and Scotland to Newhaven. By then, 100,000 cars were being carried each year by Motorail, the name used to promote the network. Services declined rapidly from the 1980s.

▼ The world's first all-line car train terminal was opened by Motorail at Kensington Olympia on 24 May 1966, offering services to many parts of Britain. There were special passenger lounges and all loading was under cover.

British Rail Car-Carrying Services 1966

Get there sooner — take your car by train

▲ Motorail used a variety of vehicles for car transport, including these standard flat trucks and dedicated two-tier carriers, photographed at Carlisle Citadel station in July 1970.

▶ A British Rail 1966 brochure includes details of all day and sleeper car-carrying services then available, most of which operated from May to September. Among the unusual routes were Sutton Coldfield to Stirling, Newton-le-Willows to Newton Abbot, Stirling or Leeds to Newhaven and York to Inverness. There were also connections with ferries to France and Ireland.

▼ This promotional card issued by the London & North Western Railway in the Edwardian era shows the early days of car carrying.

WESTERN REGION

CONVEYANCE OF MOTOR CARS

By Rail through the

SEVERN TUNNEL

Any type of private motor car capable of being loaded on standard rail vehicles will be conveyed through the Severn Tunnel at the following rates :—

	s. d.
SINGLE JOURNEY	22/6
RETURN JOURNEY	35/-

Waterproof Sheets are provided to cover cars conveyed, at a charge of 2s. 0d. per sheet.

The Trains will be limited and applications will be dealt with in strict rotation.

▲ The Great Western began to carry cars through the Severn Tunnel in 1909, and this service remained popular with drivers wanting to avoid the long route round the Severn estuary. This 1962 leaflet offered daily services.

UNLOADING MOTOR CARS AT CAMDEN GOODS STATION, OVAL ROAD, N.W.
Order and Consign "per London & North Western Railway."

ENGINE SHEDS

For any railway enthusiast in the steam age, Mecca was represented by the engine shed, a magic and mysterious place devoted to the servicing and maintenance of steam locomotives. All trainspotters visited sheds, usually unofficially but sometimes armed with that ever-so-desirable piece of paper, the Shed Pass. Apart from the excitement of the experience, a shed visit usually offered the chance to record a large number of locomotive sightings, including some unexpected rarities, and to underline their numbers in the *ABC* guides. There were hundreds of sheds spread over the railway network, making them accessible to enthusiasts even in remote corners of the country.

Steam locomotives are complicated machines demanding regular servicing and constant maintenance. The shed, or Motive Power Depot in modern parlance, enabled much of this to be carried out under cover, while at the same time offering storage for locomotives not in use. As a result, sheds emerged in the very early days of the railways. The earliest, and the most common, was the straight type, with parallel tracks and inspection pits and access from both ends. Their advantage was that they were relatively easy to construct and extend,

▲ Middlesbrough shed, seen here towards the end of its life, was an example of the semi-circular type of shed, with tracks radiating from a central turntable. Iron columns support the roof.

▼ A busy mainline shed was a constant turmoil of activity. This is Cardiff's exotically named Canton shed photographed in the early 1960s, with a variety of locomotives being prepared for duty. By now the shed was firmly in British Railway's Western Region, yet it still bore the clear stamp of the old GWR.

▲ Worcester had a linear shed, with three running tracks. In the summer of 1958 the shed was still busy. GWR 6950 'Kingsthorpe Hall' stands on shed, over the ash pit. To the left is a row of stored locomotives and to the right the ubiquitous line of coal wagons. A man with the look of an enthusiast is striding out of the shed.

BRITISH RAILWAYS—OPERATIONS DEPARTMENT

RIDING OF BICYCLES ON THE BOARD'S PREMISES

Attention has been called to the practice that has arisen of Employees riding bicycles along the railway, also in and around Engine Sheds.

All members of the staff are hereby notified that this practice is forbidden.

CHIEF OPERATIONS MANAGER

and could house a large number of locomotives. The GWR's Swindon shed of the 1840s could hold forty-eight. Linear sheds could be of any size, right down to the little ones at the ends of branch lines, designed for a single engine. The other main type was circular or semi-circular, with tracks radiating from a central turntable. These were used where space was restricted and many, such as the Roundhouse at Camden Town, in north London, were architecturally very striking. Their disadvantage was that only one locomotive at a time could use the turntable. As a result, larger sheds often had several turntables. Early sheds were built of wood, but this soon gave way to brick and stone, and later to steel and concrete. The roofs were often partially glazed, with plenty of smoke vents.

The shed itself was used mainly for storage and servicing but also associated with the shed, and its yards, were facilities for coaling, watering, ash removal and turning. A locomotive that had been through the service procedure was said to be 'on shed' and ready for use. For decades, servicing was done largely by hand but from the 1930s mechanization brought coaling towers and ash disposal

▲ Steam haulage finished on the Southern Region in July 1967. On the last day two classic Bulleid locomotives, 34060 '25 Squadron' and 34098 'Templecombe', stand silent inside Salisbury shed, their active lives over. The scrapyard beckons.

◀ By 1967 steam was clearly on the way out, yet in March that year Crewe South shed was still full of activity as the Black Fives and a Britannia were prepared for duty. This yard also boasted a mechanical coaling tower, which dominates the skyline.

▼ Deep in rural Norfolk, Melton Constable was an unlikely location for a railway works. As a meeting point for four lines, it also had a busy, and surprisingly modern, shed, as this 1950s photograph indicates.

▲ Photographs showing GWR sheds during the Victorian era are unusual. This shed's location is unknown but the identities of two locomotives can be established: 338 and 1227.

▼ This is Swindon motive power depot in the 1960s, as steam was giving way to diesel. Two old Halls lurk in the shadows, while a Western and a Type 3 Hymek take the limelight.

systems. Large central water tanks fed the many water columns around the shed and the yard. In some cases water and coaling towers were combined. Many sheds were equipped with workshops to enable basic maintenance to be carried out, while larger ones often had full facilities for major repairs and overhauls, along with offices and accommodation.

As diesel and electric locomotives began to replace steam, some sheds were adapted. However, as most were related directly to the needs of steam engines, the vast majority were closed, abandoned and often demolished. New uses were found for a few but in principle the old shed, and everything it represented, was faced with extinction. Some early or unusual roundhouses have been listed and preserved but they are no longer in use as sheds. Today the only complete large-scale steam era depot that survives in Britain, and probably in Western Europe, is Steamtown, at Carnforth, in Lancashire.

Trains still need servicing and maintaining, so a new generation of modern maintenance depots has been built by the various operating companies. Often impressive in both scale and equipment, these represent the new world of the railways in Britain, but they will never match the allure and magic of the old shed.

▲ Many sheds had occasional open days but were rarely seen as spic and span as Willesden, London, looks here, during a British Railways exhibition in June 1954.

▼ By 1972 old steam sheds were disappearing rapidly. However, some had been taken over by the diesels. This is Gateshead, with turntable still in place but disused. At least four classes of diesel are present, including a Deltic, D9011 'The Royal Northumberland Fusiliers'.

BR. 32709/4.

BRITISH RAILWAYS BOARD.

NOTICE.

JUMPING OVER INSPECTION PITS IS PROHIBITED.

▼ On 10 July 1967, the day after steam haulage ended on the Southern Region, the engine shed at Weymouth became a graveyard and dumping ground for many classes of once-proud, now redundant locomotives.

▼ Larger sheds were equipped with full repair facilities. Here, in Perth shed, in September 1961, 45483 has a major overhaul, its weight supported by the heavy lift crane.

EARLY RAILWAY CLOSURES

The major railway closure programmes that began in the early 1960s devastated the British network. As a result, it is easy to forget that line closures have always taken place, starting in the 1840s and continuing through the Victorian era. In the 1920s and 1930s, when the Big Four were struggling to come to terms with the complex and often overlapping network they had inherited, about 3,500 route miles were lost. There were also quite extensive closures during the late 1940s and the 1950s, in the early years of nationalized British Railways. However, until the 1960s, railway closures aroused little public attention, and lines disappeared largely unnoticed and unlamented. It is therefore rare to find early photographs of lost lines, taken by pioneer explorers who, at the time, must have been seen as decidedly eccentric as they trudged the fields in search of long-forgotten railways.

▲ In the early 1860s a line was opened along the Biddulph valley, connecting Stoke and Congleton. It was designed primarily to serve collieries and iron works but passengers were carried from about 1864. It was operated by the North Staffordshire Railway.

▼ In 1859 the railway reached Portsoy, Aberdeenshire, and later a branch was built down a steep incline to the harbour. By 1937, when this photograph was taken, the branch was long gone but the route could still be explored. The line to Portsoy was closed in 1963.

◀ ▶ By 1958, when these photographs of the former Stoke-to-Congleton line were taken, much had disapppeared. The photograph on the left (opposite page) shows the trackbed of the main line near Biddulph, at a junction with a branch that served a local limestone quarry. The photograph on the right shows another view of the former main line, which by 1958 was serving as an access road for garages and light industrial premises. The railway had closed some years before the car was made.

◀ In the 1950s walking old railways must have been an unusual and solitary hobby. This third view of the former Stoke-to-Congleton line shows the trackbed near the line's summit, curving its way through woodland in a shallow cutting. By this time the line had been closed for over thirty years.

The Dundee & Newtyle Railway was built during the 1820s as a horse-worked line. It had a chequered career, having little traffic but great local support. By 1933, when these five photographs were taken by AC Lowe, some of the early sections had been bypassed or replaced. Above, left to right: a bridge over the original trackbed near Auchterhouse, the old line from the new Auchterhouse station, the old summit level. Left: looking up the Hatton incline near Newtyle. Right: the original station at Newtyle, which by 1933 was in use as a goods shed. The line closed in 1955.

FORGOTTEN FREIGHT

After a slow start, goods (or, in modern terminology, freight) traffic developed rapidly. By the early 1850s it had overtaken passenger traffic in revenue terms, and remained at least 30 per cent higher until the early 1960s. In about 1912 nearly 400 million tons were being carried each year, but from that point traffic declined steadily and by the late 1960s had halved. These figures reflect the fact that there was a time when the railways carried everything, from bulk cargoes such as coal, oil, stone, agricultural produce and raw materials to livestock, food and drink, clothing, garden tools and all the varied products for the village shop. At the time, nearly every station in Britain had a goods yard, shed or even just a goods siding, with basic handling facilities. In the course of its journey, the merchandise might have to change wagons or trains several times. The movement of all this freight, and its successful delivery, required a complex system of documentation, all of which was managed by hand. Also necessary was a network of carriers, to transport the goods to the station at the start of the journey and to the final address at the end. Now, only certain bulk cargoes are carried by train. Everything else has gone on to the roads, including newspapers, mail and parcels. Only photographs and surprising amounts of surviving paperwork tell the story of the extraordinary diversity of goods traffic on the railways.

▲ Until the introduction in the 1920s of special bulk milk tankers for long-distance transport, milk was carried in metal churns. These were brought to country stations all over Britain for onward carriage. Here, a large group awaits collection from Corfe Castle, Dorset, in the 1920s.

Despatching Herrings, Lancashire & Yorkshire Rly. Co.'s Wyre Dock, Fleetwood.
FISH landed from trawlers at Wyre Dock, Fleetwood, and handed to the Lancashire & Yorkshire Railway Company, is conveyed by specially arranged services.

◀ Thanks to the railways, fishing harbours expanded rapidly and fresh fish was available all over Britain. Many railway companies ran dedicated, high-speed trains to get the fish from port to market overnight. This Edwardian card was issued by the Lancashire & Yorkshire to promote its fish trains from Fleetwood.

POULTRY, CHEESE MAKING, RABBITS, ✠ G.E.R. ○ ✈
HORTICULTURE INCLUDING BOTTLING &
CANNING OF FRUITS,
GOATS,
BEES, ALLOTMENT GARDENING.

G.E. RAILWAY Cº

▲ The railways were early users of containers. By the 1930s these were often designed for interchange between rail and road. This promotional card of that era shows an LMS version.

▲ Above right: Parcels, perishables, some livestock, smaller items and urgent goods could be sent by passenger train. This Great Eastern Railway advertising card was designed to promote these services to smallholders and allotment gardeners. On the back of the card there are tips about natural hatching and rearing of chickens, perhaps unexpected advice from a railway company.

CALEDONIAN SPECIAL TRAIN,
CONVEYING PAPER FOR GLASGOW. "EVENING NEWS."

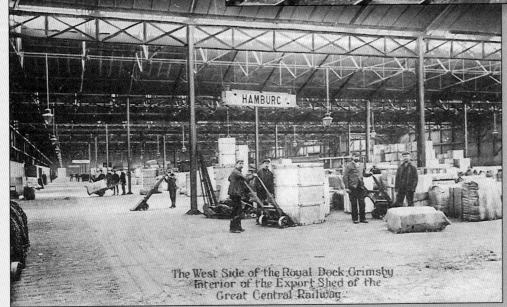

The West Side of the Royal Dock Grimsby
Interior of the Export Shed of the
Great Central Railway

▲ This colourful Edwardian card was issued by the Caledonian Railway to draw attention to its special trains carrying newsprint for the *Glasgow Evening News*. Railway publicity at the time made much of freight, and official cards such as these indicate the importance of freight services at a time when they were at their peak.

◄ International freight was also important. This Edwardian view of the export shed at Grimsby's Royal Dock was published by the Great Central Railway.

◀ Town gas was generally available in the Victorian era but there was no national distribution. Every town had its own gas works and the railway supplied the coal and took away the coke after the gas had been extracted. This is Chipping Norton, in Oxfordshire, in about 1910. The famous mill, with its tall central chimney, still stands.

▼ Railways have always been prime movers of bulk cargoes such as coal and stone, and to some extent still are. Many quarries were rail-connected and many stations had stone wharfs, or depots, such as this one at Corsham, in Wiltshire, which handled Bath stone.

CHIPPING NORTON GAS WORKS - 1

Stone Wharf, Corsham Station.

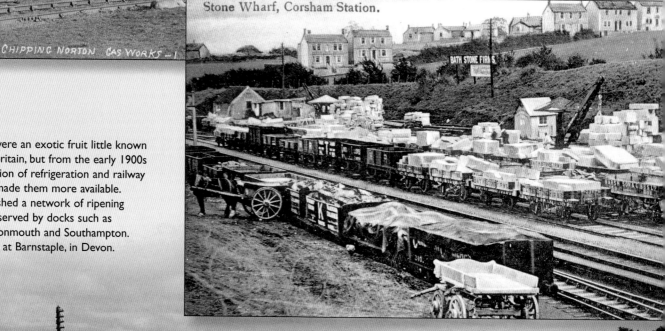

▼ Bananas were an exotic fruit little known in Victorian Britain, but from the early 1900s the combination of refrigeration and railway distribution made them more available. Fyffes established a network of ripening warehouses, served by docks such as Liverpool, Avonmouth and Southampton. This one was at Barnstaple, in Devon.

FYFFES

▶ Stratford market, in east London, was opened by the Great Eastern in 1879 for the wholesale distribution of fruit and vegetables, largely from market gardens. The railways had to cope with the demands of the changing seasons and the perishable nature of the crops, as well as ensuring both careful handling and rapid distribution.

GREAT EASTERN RAILWAY STRATFORD MARKET LONDON, E.

FRUIT, VEGETABLES, &c.,
DIRECT FROM THE FARMS.

THE MARKET IS OPEN DAILY
for the Reception and Sale of
FRUIT, POTATOES, ROOTS
AND OTHER
GENERAL FARM PRODUCE.

Particulars as to rates, accommodation, etc., may be obtained of Mr. Wm. C. MAY, Goods Manager, Liverpool Street Station, London, E.C.

▼ This view of a goods shed at Reading in about 1910 shows the complexity of the goods-handling operation that was an everyday feature of railway life until the 1960s. A line of partially loaded open wagons sits between the raised platforms while the porters work out what has to be taken on and off. They are surrounded by an extraordinary variety of goods, and the clerk at his portable desk tries to keep track of it all and prepare the necessary paperwork, upon which the whole system was entirely dependent.

L. & S. W. Ry.—LABELLED NEWSPAPER PARCELS WAY BILL.

(W. & S. Ltd.) (887) 8/00.

Guards' Signatures.

_____ Railway.

From _Wynworth_ To _Dorchester_ On the _____ 19__ Via _____

Departure _Nine_ o'clock Train _28_ day of _2_

No. of Packages.	Description.	NAME.	Weight. lbs.	Value of Labels. £ s. d.
		actor D.L.Chronicle		

◀ Newspapers were carried on trains as early as 1831 and the traffic built quickly, thanks to stationers such as WH Smith. Special newspaper trains were soon running, and London papers began to threaten the provincial press. The electric telegraph levelled the playing field, and newspapers of all kinds continued to travel by special train well into the 20th century.

Est. S. 5/10 25,000 3/32.

O. 6059

DEAD MEAT BY GOODS TRAIN

LONDON & NORTH EASTERN RAILWAY.

Date _4/10_

From _BISHOPSGATE GOODS_

TO _CLACTON_

_____ SECTION _____ COY.

VIA _____

Consignee _____

Owner and No of Wagon _165923_

Contents _____ Quantity _____

◀ Refrigerated and ventilated wagons came into service from the 1880s.

▼ Some large goods depots had bonded warehouses that had to conform to Customs and Excise regulations, which also applied to wines, spirits and cigarettes being transported by train. In addition, many Scottish whisky distilleries were rail-connected.

LMS. _74/14_ _4-50_ _10 HHDS WHISKY_ E.R.O. 33815

UNDER BOND

To COLLECTOR OF H.M. CUSTOMS & EXCISE

NO 1 BOND

BATHURST WHARF

Description of Traffic _BRISTOL_

FROM _BRITISH RAILWAYS BOARD_

149 BELL ST.

GLASGOW, C.4.

CONS SAINSBURY BROS.

▼ The universality of railway freight transport is reflected by special paperwork for unusual cargoes such as theatrical luggage.

MIDLAND RAILWAY.

CONSIGNMENT NOTE FOR THEATRICAL LUGGAGE, &c.

The Midland Railway Company hereby give notice that in lieu of the ordinary rates of charge and conditions of carriage, they are willing, at the sender's option to carry the personal luggage, costumes, scenery, and other usual equipment of theatrical and equestrian companies and other public entertainers by passenger trains at owner's risk, when such baggage is accompanied by the persons owning or using the same, at the following special rates of charge, viz.:—

3 cwts. for each 1st class passenger } free of charge.
1½ „ „ 3rd „ „ }

Weights in excess of the above ...... half the rates ordinarily charged by the Company for excess luggage.

In consideration of your receiving and forwarding the undermentioned goods at the above-named special rates of charge, I agree, on behalf of the respective persons owning or using the same, to relieve you and all other Companies or persons over whose lines the goods may pass, or in whose possession the same may be during any portion of the transit, from all liability for loss, damage, or delay from whatever cause arising. This agreement shall be deemed to be separately made with each Company or person over whose lines the goods may pass, or in whose possession the same may be during any portion of the transit.

Name of sender _____

Address _____

Signature of sender }
or representative } _____

Name of sender.	Station to which goods are to be sent.	No. of passengers in party.		No. of articles or packages.	Description of goods.
		1st class.	3rd class		

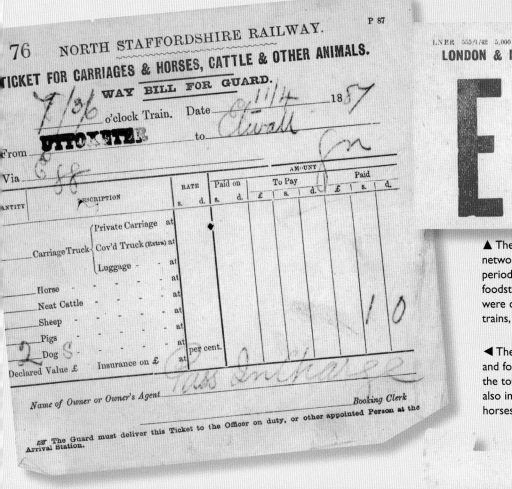

76 **P 87**
NORTH STAFFORDSHIRE RAILWAY.
TICKET FOR CARRIAGES & HORSES, CATTLE & OTHER ANIMALS.

WAY BILL FOR GUARD.

o'clock Train. Date _11/4_ 18_57_

from _UTTOXETER_ to _Etwall_

Via

QUANTITY	DESCRIPTION	RATE s. d.	Paid on s. d.	To Pay £ s. d.	Paid £ s. d.
	Private Carriage at				
	Carriage Truck · Cov'd Truck (Extra) at				
	Luggage - at				
	- at				
	Horse - at				
	Neat Cattle - at				
	Sheep - at				
	Pigs - at			1 0	
2	Dog S at per cent.				
	Declared Value £ Insurance on £ at				

Name of Owner or Owner's Agent

Booking Clerk

☞ The Guard must deliver this Ticket to the Officer on duty, or other appointed Person at the Arrival Station.

L.N.E.R. 555/1/42 5,000

LONDON & NORTH EASTERN RAILWAY   P. 3055

EGGS

▲ The comprehensive nature of the railway network meant that it was well placed over a long period for the carriage of perishable and delicate foodstuffs, notably eggs and dairy products. Eggs were often carried in the guard's vans of passenger trains, in special protective boxes.

◀ The movement of animals from farm to market, and for slaughter, was a huge business: in 1913, the total was nearly 20 million animals. Horses were also important, with special horseboxes for race horses, complete with groom's compartment.

Lancashire & Yorkshire Railway.

M 88 Date _26/8/05_
GRAIN
From WAKEFIELD HOIST,

To _Knottingley_

Via _by C_

Owner & No. of Wagon

Owner & No. of Sheet

Owner & No. of Under Sheet

Consignee

▲ Grain, wheat, hay, straw and many other bulk agricultural products, such as sugar beet, potatoes, cabbages and cauliflowers and, significantly, fertilizers, were important cargoes over a long period. In fact, the railways revolutionized the farming industry in many ways.

▶ The carriage of flowers in special wagons attached to express passenger and parcels trains was important from the 1880s, with several hundred tons being carried each year, mainly from Cornwall and ports serving the Channel Islands. This leaflet shows the traffic was still thriving in the early 1960s.

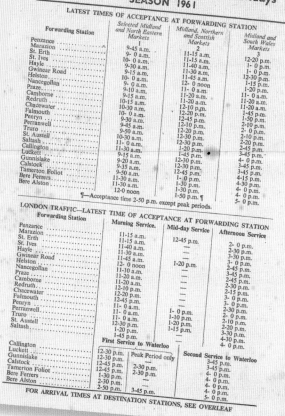

BRITISH RAILWAYS

Flower Traffic by Express Passenger and Parcels Services from Cornwall and Devon—Weekdays
SEASON 1961
LATEST TIMES OF ACCEPTANCE AT FORWARDING STATION

Forwarding Station	Selected Midland and North Eastern Markets 1	Midland, Northern and Scottish Markets 2	Midland and South Wales Markets 3
Penzance			
Marazion	9-45 a.m.	11-15 a.m.	12-20 p.m.
St. Erth	9- 0 a.m.	11-15 a.m.	1- 0 p.m.
St. Ives	10- 0 a.m.	11-40 a.m.	
Hayle	9-30 a.m.	11-30 a.m.	1- 0 p.m.
Gwinear Road	9-15 a.m.	11-45 a.m.	12-30 p.m.
Helston	10- 0 a.m.	12- 0 noon	1-15 p.m.
Nancegollan	9- 0 a.m.	11- 0 a.m.	11- 0 a.m.
Praze	9-10 a.m.	11-20 a.m.	1-20 p.m.
Camborne	9-15 a.m.		11-20 a.m.
Redruth	10-15 a.m.	11-20 a.m.	11-20 a.m.
Chacewater	10-30 a.m.	12-10 p.m.	1-45 p.m.
Falmouth	10- 0 a.m.	12-20 p.m.	1-50 p.m.
Penryn	9-30 a.m.	12-45 p.m.	2-10 p.m.
Perranwell	9-45 a.m.	12-10 p.m.	2- 0 p.m.
Truro	9-50 a.m.	12-20 p.m.	2- 0 p.m.
St. Austell	10-30 a.m.	12-30 p.m.	2-10 p.m.
Saltash	11- 0 a.m.	12-30 p.m.	2-20 p.m.
Callington	11-30 a.m.	1- 20 p.m.	2-45 p.m.
Luckett	9-15 a.m.	1-45 p.m.	3-45 p.m.
Gunnislake	9-20 a.m.	12-30 p.m.	3-45 p.m.
Calstock	9-25 a.m.	12-45 p.m.	3-45 p.m.
Tamerton Foliot	9-50 a.m.	1- 0 p.m.	4-15 p.m.
Bere Ferrers	11-30 a.m.	1-30 p.m.	4-30 p.m.
Bere Alston	11-30 a.m.	1-30 p.m.	4- 0 p.m.
	12-0 noon	1-50 p.m.	4- 0 p.m.

¶—Acceptance time 2-50 p.m. except peak periods.

LONDON TRAFFIC—LATEST TIME OF ACCEPTANCE AT FORWARDING STATION

Forwarding Station	Morning Service.	Mid-day Service	Afternoon Service
Penzance			
Marazion	11-15 a.m.		
St. Erth	11-15 a.m.	12-45 p.m.	
Hayle	11-40 a.m.		2- 0 p.m.
Gwinear Road	11-30 a.m.		2-30 p.m.
Helston	11-45 a.m.		3- 0 p.m.
Nancegollan	12- 0 noon	1-20 p.m.	2- 0 p.m.
Praze	11-10 a.m.		2-45 p.m.
Camborne	11-20 a.m.		3-45 p.m.
Redruth	11-20 a.m.		2-45 p.m.
Chacewater	12-10 p.m.		2- 0 p.m.
Falmouth	12-20 p.m.		2-15 p.m.
Penryn	11- 0 a.m.		3- 0 p.m.
Perranwell	11- 0 a.m.		2-30 p.m.
Truro	11- 0 a.m.	1- 0 p.m.	2- 0 p.m.
St. Austell	12-30 p.m.	1-10 p.m.	2-10 p.m.
Saltash	1-45 p.m.	1-20 p.m.	2- 0 p.m.
		1-15 p.m.	4-30 p.m.

	First Service to Waterloo		Second Service to Waterloo
Callington	12-30 p.m.	Peak Period only	
Luckett	12-30 p.m.		3-45 p.m.
Gunnislake	12-45 p.m.	2-30 p.m.	3-45 p.m.
Calstock	12-45 p.m.	2-30 p.m.	4- 0 p.m.
Tamerton Foliot	1-30 p.m.		4- 0 p.m.
Bere Ferrers	2-30 p.m.		4- 0 p.m.
Bere Alston	2-50 p.m.	3-45 p.m.	4- 0 p.m.

FOR ARRIVAL TIMES AT DESTINATION STATIONS, SEE OVERLEAF

LOST RAILWAY COMPANIES

T he railway network of Britain was constructed in a piecemeal way by hundreds of independent companies, mainly during the Victorian era. Some were set up to build major trunk routes linking the industrial and population centres of Britain, while others were entirely local affairs, raising money to construct the few miles of track that would link their town or village to the main network. Whatever their size or ambition, all were united by their belief in the social and economic power of the railway. Some were successful, others failed. Some small ones were short-lived, and were soon swallowed up by their larger neighbours. By the end of the 19th century the major companies dominated the network, but many minor ones retained their independence until the 1923 Grouping, when the vast majority were absorbed into the Big Four – GWR, SR, LMS and LNER. The greatest survival from the years of independence is paperwork. Every company, however small, had its own look, its own style, its own paperwork. These documents, still surprisingly accessible to collectors, are a memorial to railway diversity.

▲ The Bristol & Exeter was an early broad-gauge line completed in 1844. By absorbing other companies, it eventually operated a network of more than 200 miles. It was taken over itself by the GWR in 1876, having already been converted to standard gauge.

▲ The original main line of the North British Railway from Berwick to Edinburgh opened in 1846. It expanded steadily by taking over other companies and, by the time it was absorbed into the LNER, its network included over fifty railways. In 1878 it opened the notorious Tay bridge.

◀ The Brecon & Merthyr Tydfil Junction Railway was authorized between 1859 and 1862, and its route was completed in 1868. It remained independent until 1922, when it was absorbed into the GWR. Its route, closed in 1964, contained the highest tunnel in Britain, at 1312ft.

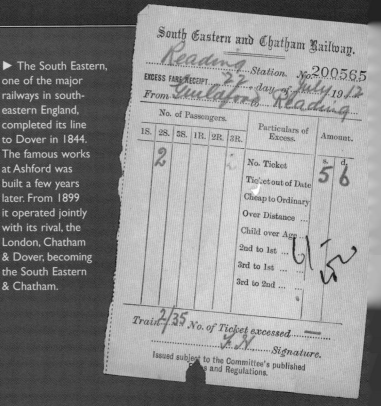

INWARD GOODS.

No. 4

DUNDEE AND ARBROATH JOINT RAILWAY.—Goods Department.

STATION, 12/6/9?

have Carted out from the Station, for delivery,

| Tons. | Cwts. | Qrs. | Lbs. |

Weighing...... : 5 :   Consigned to

For which Cartage is charged by the Railway Company.

Number of Smalls,   Empties,

Carter.   Weigher.

► The South Eastern, one of the major railways in south-eastern England, completed its line to Dover in 1844. The famous works at Ashford was built a few years later. From 1899 it operated jointly with its rival, the London, Chatham & Dover, becoming the South Eastern & Chatham.

South Eastern and Chatham Railway.

Reading Station. No. 200565

EXCESS FARE RECEIPT. 27 day of July 1912

From Guildford to Reading

No. of Passengers.						Particulars of Excess.	Amount.
1S.	2S.	3S.	1R.	2R.	3R.		s. d.
	2					No. Ticket	5 6
						Ticket out of Date	
						Cheap to Ordinary	
						Over Distance ...	
						Child over Age ...	
						2nd to 1st ...	
						3rd to 1st ...	
						3rd to 2nd ...	

Train 2/35 No. of Ticket excessed ......—

J.N. Signature.

Issued subject to the Committee's published Rules and Regulations.

▲ The Dundee & Arbroath was opened in 1840, built to a 5ft 6in gauge, and it remained isolated until 1848. Later, in 1880, it became part of the Caledonian and North British networks.

▼ The Somerset & Dorset Railway completed its line in 1874 but financial problems meant that it was operated from 1875 jointly by the LSWR and the Midland.

LANCASTER AND CARLISLE RAILWAY.

CASTLE STATION, LANCASTER, NOV. 1853.

CAUTION TO BREAKSMEN.

Every breaksman in charge of a train, shall before starting, carefully examine the break of his van, to see that it is in good order, well oiled, and that all the pins and cotters are properly secured. Any breaksman neglecting this order will be fined

South Western & Midland Railway Companies'
Somerset & Dorset Joint Line.

(492)

INSURED.

(No.   )

From

To

Train

Date

187

▲ The Lancaster & Carlisle's expensive and demanding route was completed in 1846 but it soon became part of the LNWR's west coast main line from London to Scotland.

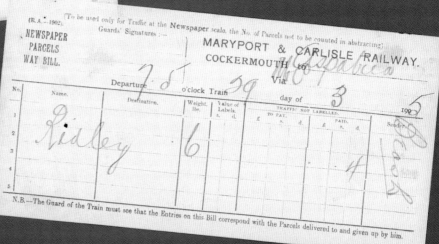

(R.A. 1902)   (To be used only for Traffic at the Newspaper scale, the No. of Parcels not to be counted in abstracting)
Guards' Signatures :—

NEWSPAPER PARCELS WAY BILL.

MARYPORT & CARLISLE RAILWAY.
COCKERMOUTH to
Via

Departure 7 5 o'clock Train 39   day of 3

No.	Name.	Destination.	Weight. lbs.	Value of Labels. £ s. d.	TRAFFIC NOT LABELLED. TO PAY. £ s. d.	PAID. £ s. d.	Sender.
1	Ridley		6				
2							
3							
4							
5							

N.B.—The Guard of the Train must see that the Entries on this Bill correspond with the Parcels delivered to and given up by him.

► After a lengthy and tortuous gestation, the Maryport & Carlisle opened its 28-mile route in 1845. It then managed to remain independent until 1923.

EAST ANGLIA

LOST & FOUND

THERE ARE NO STRAIGHT LINES in nature, even in East Anglia. Near Guestwick, north of Norwich, an old embankment forms the horizon.

◀ THE LITTLE NORTH NORFOLK village of Melton Constable became for a century an industrial town, thanks to the Midland & Great Northern's locomotive works. Today little remains but the great works water tower, its panels clearly stamped M&GN.

▶ CLARE STATION, IN SUFFOLK, a handsome building in brick and stone, survives with its platforms and goods shed as a feature in a country park. In use until the 1960s, it was famous as the only station in Britain to be built within the walls of a medieval castle.

▼ A WELL-DEFINED TRACK crosses the broad landscape towards the horizon near Heacham, south-east of Hunstanton. Only the low embankment reveals that this was the railway line to Wells-next-the-Sea.

▶ MANY RURAL BRANCH LINES have largely vanished but there is always something to prove they were once there. Near Yaxley, on the short Eye branch in Suffolk, a stretch of trackbed and a brick bridge tell the story.

PETERBOROUGH TO KING'S LYNN

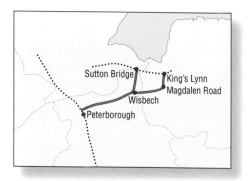

The low-lying landscape of Lincolnshire and north Cambridgeshire encouraged the building of railways and, until the 1960s, a dense network served the region, with some inevitable duplication. Typical were the two routes from Peterborough to Wisbech and King's Lynn. The more direct was a line completed in 1866, linking Peterborough and Sutton Bridge via Wisbech. At Sutton Bridge it met the line to King's Lynn, while from Wisbech there was another, older route via Watlington (or Magdalen Road, as it became), built originally as a branch by the Lynn & Ely Railway. Mergers brought the two routes into different ownership but all became part of the LNER and then British Railways, until closure in the 1960s. The landscape that made the railways easy to build also made them easy to remove, with the result that today there is little to be seen. The trackbed is visible in places, for example east of Peterborough, but has largely been ploughed out. Stations do survive, with Ferry, Tydd, Emneth, Smeeth Road and Middle Drove all recognizable, but mostly now private houses. The section from Wisbech to Sutton Bridge is a footpath along the Nene, but nothing else can really be walked. However, the dedicated explorer will find other traces, notably bridges, a couple of which are surprisingly substantial survivors.

Train Leaving G. E. Station, Peterboro'. P.S.

▲ Peterborough had several stations but the starting point for this route was Peterborough East, shown in this Edwardian postcard with a train ready to depart.

▶ At Murrow the line to Wisbech crossed the line from March to Spalding on the level and there were two stations, West and East. This is East, on the Wisbech line. Today, traces of the former junction can be seen, including a goods shed.

MURROW. MID. & G.N. STATION.

The Steam Tram, Elm Road, Wisbech.

◀ Wisbech had a complicated railway history, with three stations, serving three lines, and the little steam tramway to Upwell, seen here in about 1910 at the start of its line, by Wisbech East station.

▼ The stations between Wisbech and King's Lynn on the former branch from Watlington were quite distinctive, as this 1920s view of Emneth shows. Note the old carriage body behind the platform, probably used as a store.

▼ Remarkably, several stations on the Wisbech-to-Watlington section survive as private houses, though the track has generally vanished. This is Emneth. The carriage parked in the garden echoes the old photograph above.

▲ Much of the former route from Wisbech towards Sutton Bridge can be walked, with the wide Nene flowing beyond the embankment on the right. This is the view along the trackbed towards the remarkably remote Ferry station, now a private house.

▼ The vast majority of the trackbed has simply been ploughed back into the fields but traces do remain. This old concrete bridge over a stream survives near Smeeth Road, completely isolated and surrounded by fields of cabbages and other crops.

◄ The line had few engineering features and most were removed long ago. Two large bridges do survive, rather unexpectedly, though with no trackbed to connect them. This one crosses the Middle Level Main Drain. From the other, across the Hundred Foot Drain, the old embankment curved away towards Watlington.

► A busy port and major railway centre until the 1960s, King's Lynn was, and still is, a town with a great architectural heritage, as this 1950s card of the Old Customs House shows.

▼ Watlington, or Magdalen Road as it was from the 1870s, is still a station on the main line from Cambridge to King's Lynn. It looks not unlike this 1950s photograph. The old junction with the Wisbech line was to the south of the station.

MID-SUFFOLK LIGHT RAILWAY

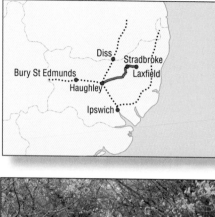

Railway fever gripped Britain in the first half of the 19th century. There were triumphs and disasters but much of the national network was built relatively quickly. By the 1880s most things were in place though minor additions continued to be made. However, the passing of the Light Railways Act in 1896 gave a new impetus to railway building, particularly in rural areas. Light railways did not need crossing gates, complex signalling or even platforms, but speeds were limited to 25mph. Typical of those built under the Act was the Mid-Suffolk Light Railway, whose planned line between Haughley and Halesworth, on the Lowestoft line via Beccles, with a long branch south to Westerfield, near Ipswich, was approved in 1901. With great ceremony, the first sod was cut at Westerfield on 3 May 1902, though the railway was destined never to get that far. In 1904 the section between Haughley East and Laxfield was opened by a company with strong local support and its own locomotives. Money problems soon affected the line and brought work to a standstill in 1907. At that point, the main line had continued for a couple of miles beyond Laxfield to Cratfield, while the branch had reached Debenham. The railway, designed to serve a remote part of Suffolk, had depended on its connections with other lines, none of which were to be realized. It became instead a rural branch line serving nowhere in particular. Somehow it survived as an independent company until absorbed by the LNER in 1924. By the late 1940s there were two trains a day, usually mixed passenger and freight, so no one was surprised when passenger services ceased in 1952.

▲ Very little of the trackbed remains, though a short stretch exists as an official footpath between two minor roads west of Medmenham. This reveals the basic, and thus impermanent, nature of the line's original construction.

▼ The supports of an old bridge and a tall embankment mark the route of the line as it swung away from Haughley East, at the start of its 19-mile journey to nowhere.

► The exploration of old railways, even ones that have gone almost without trace, can still spring surprises. This former GER carriage, which may have run on the Mid-Suffolk line, stands abandoned in a field near Medmenham. Formerly used as a cottage, it is now clearly on its last legs.

▼ From Haughley there were nine stations, all serving small places and built in a rather rudimentary way from corrugated iron. This gave the line a distinctive look. This is Mendlesham, probably in the 1930s. Note the decorative iron lettering on the nameboard. All to be seen today is a street named Old Station Road.

Lightly constructed and with no engineering features of note, the line has now largely vanished back into the Suffolk farmland. However, there are things to be seen, including the remains of bridges near Haughley and a section of trackbed used as a footpath west of Mendlesham. Other short bits of the trackbed can be seen occasionally from minor roads, but it is impossible to trace the route in any conventional sense and it has mostly disappeared from the Ordnance Survey map. All that remains in Medmenham is a sign saying Old Station Road, but the site of Aspall & Thorndon station is still identifiable, as are some bridge supports and a section of embankment on the branch near Debenham. West of Laxfield there is the site of a crossing, with the keeper's cottage, and from here the trackbed, no more than a farm track, swings across the fields towards the village. At Brockford & Wetheringsett the Mid-Suffolk Light Railway comes briefly back to life, with a rebuilt and fully restored station and other buildings, a museum and a few hundred yards of relaid track. Trains do run and there is a collection of mainly Great Eastern Railway rolling stock.

▲ The Mid-Suffolk Light Railway was cheaply built across farmland, so it was quickly and easily returned to that farmland after it closed. As a result, few stretches of identifiable trackbed remain, making its route hard to follow. A good place is the site of Aspall & Thorndon station, typically one that served nowhere in particular, not even a village. Yet the site survives, along with something that may have been a platform. Across the road the trackbed sets off through the trees. It does not look like a railway but in Mid-Suffolk terms this is a major survivor.

▲ The Mid-Suffolk closed in 1952 and much of it quickly disappeared. However, some things did survive for a surprisingly long time. This is Horham station in 1977, under inspection by a smartly dressed young man, wearing the flared trousers of that era. He is clearly not the typical railway enthusiast.

◄ Laxfield is today a quiet rural village and in 1919, when this card was sent, it was even more so. Sadly, the highlights depicted here do not include the railway station.

LOST STATIONS: EAST ANGLIA

Eastern England, though predominantly rural, was well served by railways. Essex and Suffolk had a generous network of country and branch lines but even better was Norfolk, thanks to the meandering tentacles of the Midland & Great Northern making most of the county accessible. King's Lynn and Cambridge were major rail centres, with connections through to many other parts of England. Though often remote and little used, the stations of the region were delightfully varied, reflecting in many cases the diverse, and often competitive, nature of the railways that had built them. For the same reason, a number of places had more than one station, for example Aylsham, North Walsham, Cromer, Haverhill and Wisbech. Inevitably such railway richness in a country region was too good to last, and when the closures came they were extreme. The majority of the network was swept away in the 1960s, regardless of the social impact, and large areas, and some substantial towns, were left with no railway service at all. Many stations, great and small, disappeared and with them went much of the character and individuality that made the region so distinctive. Here is a selection to give a flavour of what has been lost.

▼ Caister Camp Halt was one of a number of minimal stations in north Norfolk. On the M&GN line from North Walsham to Yarmouth Beach, it served the nearby holiday camp. Here, in LNER days, a jolly group of holidaymakers poses in front of a railmotor.

► Glemsford was a typically rural station on the Suffolk line from Sudbury to Haverhill, quite substantial for the little place it served. There was a signal box and a goods shed, and when this picture was taken, perhaps in the 1930s, it all looked neat and tidy.

▼ Norwich had four stations. This is the grand façade of Norwich City, the terminus for the M&GN. Behind the classical opulence the station was actually quite small — but city stations had to make an impact.

▲ Hadleigh station was opened in 1847, a decorative building that reflected the local pride that had brought the railway to this small Suffolk town. Frederick Barnes was the architect and he must have relished putting so much detail into a small terminus station. Despite this, it lost its passenger trains early, in 1932, and the branch finally closed in the 1960s. The building survives.

▶ The line south from Bury St Edmunds to Long Melford was closed in May 1961, and so came the end for Lavenham, seen here in its last months. Clearly, the diesel railcar did not bring the hoped-for increase in traffic.

▼ Sutton Bridge, seen here in the 1930s, was an important junction station on the M&GN's main line west towards Peterborough, adjacent to the famous 1897 swing bridge. The station has gone but the bridge lives on, carrying cars.

LOST JOURNEY: HUNSTANTON TO MALDON

The East Anglian network was remarkably extensive, and there were many ways across the region. However, there were few main lines, and journeys on stopping trains that catered largely for local traffic were slow. This journey, from a popular resort in north-west Norfolk to an old fishing port on the Essex coast, was typical, and might have been made by a family returning from holiday or from a visit to friends. There were several possible routes, via Cambridge, Bury St Edmunds or Norwich. In this case, the choice was for the meandering M&GN network to Melton Constable and thence to Norwich, as this allowed for a brief meeting with a friend in Melton. Overall, there were five changes in a journey that took all day, passing through the varied landscape of Norfolk, Suffolk and Essex. The 1960s saw the closure of most East Anglian lines, and all that remains of the journey now is the main line from Norwich to Witham.

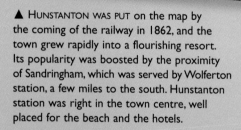

G.E.R. Station, Hunstanton. Photo May Bone.

▲ HUNSTANTON WAS PUT ON the map by the coming of the railway in 1862, and the town grew rapidly into a flourishing resort. Its popularity was boosted by the proximity of Sandringham, which was served by Wolferton station, a few miles to the south. Hunstanton station was right in the town centre, well placed for the beach and the hotels.

▶ THE RAILWAY ARRIVED in King's Lynn in the 1840s and the town soon became a major railway centre, the hub of lines radiating in five directions and into the docks. Three stations served the town but it was some distance from the main station to South Lynn, so on this journey a taxi was necessary to make the connection, and there was no time to explore.

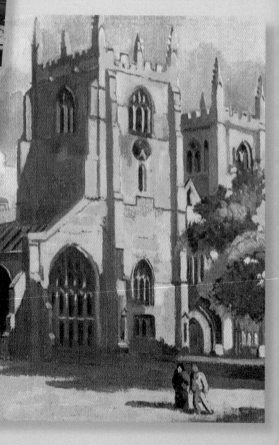

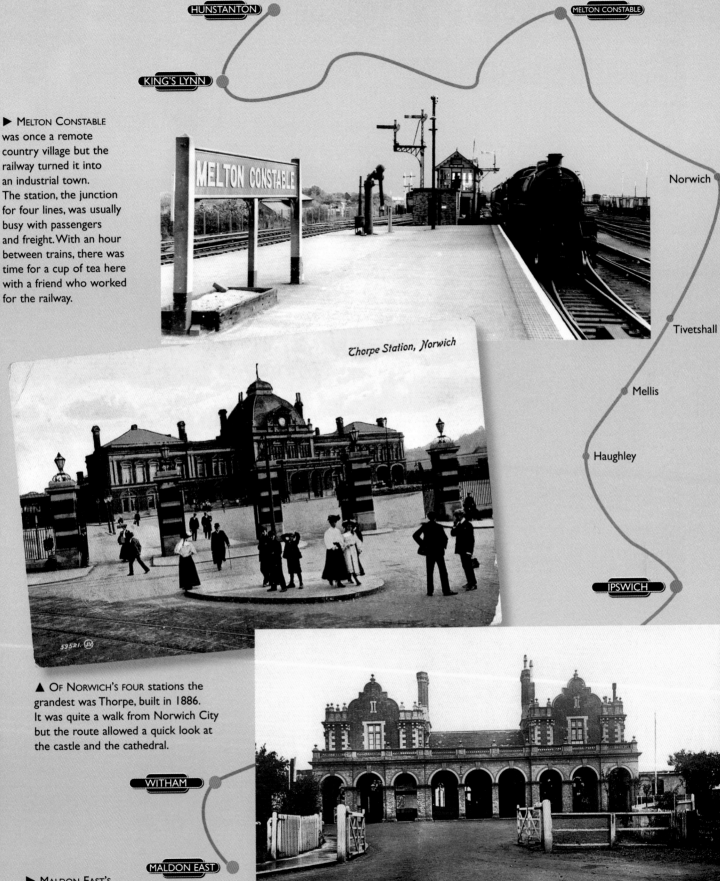

HUNSTANTON

MELTON CONSTABLE

KING'S LYNN

► MELTON CONSTABLE
was once a remote
country village but the
railway turned it into
an industrial town.
The station, the junction
for four lines, was usually
busy with passengers
and freight. With an hour
between trains, there was
time for a cup of tea here
with a friend who worked
for the railway.

Norwich

Tivetshall

Mellis

Haughley

IPSWICH

Thorpe Station, Norwich

▲ OF NORWICH'S FOUR stations the
grandest was Thorpe, built in 1886.
It was quite a walk from Norwich City
but the route allowed a quick look at
the castle and the cathedral.

WITHAM

MALDON EAST

► MALDON EAST'S
1840s Jacobean splendour made it
one of the best branchline termini in
Britain, and a fitting end to the journey.
It closed in 1964, but the building survives.

Maldon. East Station.

▲ The Great Central was Britain's last major railway. Its main route, from the Midlands to London, opened in 1899.

▲ The Mersey Docks & Harbour Board operated about 60 miles of lines around Liverpool and Birkenhead, in conjunction with the LNWR and the Great Central.

▲ When the North Eastern Railway was formed in 1854 by the merger of four local companies, its 720-mile network was the largest in Britain. The great York station was at its heart. The railway retained its independence until 1923, when it became part of the LNER.

◀ The Furness Railway, famous for haematite and tourism, remained independent from 1846 to 1923.

▲ Formed from 1865 by various companies, including the Great Northern and the Midland, the Cheshire Lines Committee operated independently in the Liverpool and Manchester region until 1923.

Formed in 1847 by the merging of several local companies, the Manchester, Sheffield & Lincolnshire gradually expanded across the country. In 1899 it built a new line to London, becoming the Great Central Railway.

On 1 January 1948 the nationalized British Railways came into being. At that point all major independent railway companies ceased to exist. History and tradition disappeared with the loss of famous names such as the GWR.

In 1881 the Hoylake & Birkenhead Tramway gave itself this grand new name, which it then enjoyed for ten years before being absorbed into the Wirral Railway.

On January 1, 1948, the Great Western Railway ceased to exist.

LOCOMOTIVES

The stars of railway history are the locomotives, astonishing in their diversity and representative in their progressive development of the imagination and engineering skills of generations of designers. Although there were famous precursors, the story really starts with Stephenson's 'Rocket', the machine that in its structure and performance determined the future of the steam locomotive. The great Victorian locomotive engineers, from Stephenson and Gooch to Stroudley, Stirling, Adams, Webb and Drummond, all advanced the process of locomotive design but the real potential of the steam engine was realized in the 20th century, in the work of men such as Churchward, Stanier, Gresley and Bulleid. Railway companies in Britain were often idiosyncratic and independently minded, and this encouraged the progress of engineering technology through experimentation. At the same time, developments within the industry tended to spread from one company to another, so many broadly similar designs were put into production. Each generation produced its classics, locomotives to feature in any enthusiast's 'Desert Island Discs' choice.

▲ The history of Britain's railways is littered with might-have-beens. A notable example is the tilting Advanced Passenger Train, which was designed to operate on existing track at up to 150mph. Initial trials in the early 1980s were unsuccessful and it was abandoned.

◄ D1001 'Western Pathfinder' leaves Paddington in 1975. For many people, the idiosyncratic Western Region class 52 was a classic diesel.

▼ A popular classic, streamlined Merchant Navy class Pacific, 34024 'East Asiatic Company', from the series designed for the Southern Railway by Oliver Bulleid, is seen here in a 1949 British Railways publicity shot.

◀ In the last years of steam, unusual pairings of locomotives were not uncommon, especially on goods trains. At Dalrymple Junction in March 1966, a Black Five and a Birmingham Railway Carriage & Wagon Works Type 2 – steam and diesel, the old and the new – work in tandem on a Stranraer-to-Glasgow train.

◀ A young enthusiast at Edinburgh admires a Victorian classic, a 4-4-0 passenger locomotive designed for the Caledonian Railway by Dugald Drummond in the 1880s. In a remarkably active career, Drummond worked for several major railways including the Highland, the North British, the London & South Western, and the London, Brighton & South Coast.

▶ The Manchester-to-Sheffield line through the Pennines was one of the first to be converted to electric power from overhead catenary cables. A 1500-volt DC system was used, following French practice, and from the 1950s a class of special locomotives was built for this route at Gorton. Two are seen here at Guide Bridge in the 1970s. The line was closed in 1981 and the locomotives died with it, as by then British Rail was using a different type of overhead power.

◀ The experimental application of turbine power to locomotives goes back to 1910. Both the LMS and the GWR tested turbine locomotives, in the 1930s and the 1950s, with limited success. One of the final experiments was GT3, an English Electric gas turbine-powered mechanical locomotive, seen here on trial passing through Ashby Magna station, on the Great Central line in Leicestershire, in September 1961.

Until the 1950s, steam was king, relatively unchallenged despite the availability of alternative power sources, notably electricity and oil, since the Edwardian period. One reason was cost, for steam locomotives were always cheaper to build. Even in the 1950s, a diesel-electric locomotive cost three times as much as a comparable steam engine. Nonetheless, British Railways determined in the late 1950s to rely in the future on diesel and electric traction, and in 1968 steam finally disappeared from the national network. Diesel and electric locomotives have gone through the same process of development and improvement, ensuring that some types, in their turn, became classics. As with steam locomotives, there have also been plenty of problems and failures along the way.

Thanks to museum collections and preserved railways, the history of the steam locomotive is well known. Many important, and unimportant, types are available for inspection, and hundreds are still in use on private lines. Diesel and

▲ Sentinel produced a successful range of steam railcars, which were used in various parts of Britain. This one was working on The Dyke branch near Brighton in the 1930s.

▲ The 1896 Light Railways Act opened the door to a new kind of railway that was meant to be cheap to build and to operate. Typical was the Kent & East Sussex Railway, which opened in 1905. Colonel Stephens was in charge, and among his cost-saving ideas in the 1920s was the use of Ford petrol-engined railcars.

▶ The short Wantage Tramway linked the town to the GWR main line, from the 1870s until its final closure in 1945. This roadside line used various locomotives, including no. 6, this typical tram engine.

◀ Steam railcars and auto-trains begin to be used extensively in the Edwardian era, with many companies developing their own designs for rural routes and branch lines. This postcard shows a Great Western 'steam motor carriage' of that period.

GREAT WESTERN RLY., STEAM MOTOR CARRIAGE. (For Working Short Branch Lines.)

The Knight Series, No. 981.

▶ In an attempt to reduce costs and keep open uneconomic routes, British Railways introduced diesel-powered railbuses in the 1950s, some purchased from independent makers. This contemporary BR postcard was issued to promote their use.

10505. Diesel Railbus "Craigendoran." British Railways Photo.

▼ Small petrol-engined locomotives were used extensively on narrow-gauge lines during World War I, and one of the major manufacturers was Simplex. The same company built standard-gauge shunting locomotives for use in depots and goods yards and on industrial lines. Some survived into the British Railways era.

electric locomotives are now following the same route, particularly as the era of locomotive-hauled passenger trains draws to a close. Not to be forgotten for their important role in the story are the auto-trains, railcars and multiple units, diesel or electric, which for decades were the mainstay of rural routes and branch lines. For most locomotives, the story was much the same: an active life of thirty or forty years, followed by relegation to minor duties or storage and then the scrapyard. Some, for no particular reason, had longer lives before being scrapped. Others that were very famous, or had simply survived, were scheduled for preservation. This was, however, an arbitrary process that resulted in both duplication and gaps. The vast majority of locomotives were simply cut up.

▲ In 1981 the two cab sections from class 31 diesel no. 31005 could be seen stacked together at Doncaster.

◄ Locomotives were cut up in railway works and by independent scrapyards. Here, class Q6 no. 63383 meets its end in the wooded surroundings of Darlington North Road.

▼ Sooner or later, every locomotive is withdrawn from service and usually is scrapped soon after. This is the skeleton of a once-proud class 46 diesel at Swindon in 1983.

▼ By 1962 destruction rather than creation was increasingly the rule at Swindon. Here, only the chassis remains of one of the great Kings, among the GWR's most famous locos.

▲ By 1963 steam locomotives were being withdrawn in large numbers and cutting up was usually done quickly to save space at the main works, such as Eastleigh.

NARROW-GAUGE LINES

T he early railway builders used many gauges, to suit the needs of local industries. It was not until the 1860s that narrow gauge, that is to say 3ft or less, became established as a viable alternative to standard gauge. Reduced construction and operating costs, particularly in difficult terrain, added to the appeal of the narrow-gauge railway. Wales became the home of narrow gauge, even though the gauge itself was far from standard (2ft, 2ft 3in, 2ft 8in and 3ft were all in use). Lines were primarily industrial, for the transport of slate and other minerals, and passenger traffic was largely unimportant. In England the national network was by then so comprehensive that there was little demand for narrow-gauge except in local industries such as clay or stone. Later the rise of tourism and the passing, in 1896, of the Light Railways Act prompted a new enthusiasm for passenger-carrying narrow-gauge lines, with more than ten opening in various parts of Britain between the 1890s and the 1920s. At the same time, existing industrial lines turned themselves into tourist railways. In this new role, narrow-gauge railways flourished until the 1930s, when most went out of business.

▲ One of Britain's most remote narrow-gauge lines was the Campbeltown & Machrihanish in Scotland. Originally a coal line, it was rebuilt for passengers in 1906. It was never very successful, despite attractive publicity such as this card, and closed in 1932.

◀ Encouraged by Southwold Town Council, keen to bring visitors to its developing little resort, the Southwold Railway opened in 1879, with four trains a day linking with the main line at Halesworth. It prospered until the 1920s, when increasing competition from road transport brought it to an end in 1929.

◀ Dinorwic was one of the largest of the Welsh slate quarries, served by an extensive narrow-gauge network and with mainline connections at Port Dinorwic. Slate wagons were hauled between quarry levels by inclined planes.

▶ Opened in 1859 to serve slate quarries in the hills above Machynlleth, the Corris developed in the 1880s an early interest in passenger-carrying. It also pioneered connecting bus services. Taken over by the GWR in 1930, it lost its passenger services in 1931 but freight traffic continued until 1948.

▼ In this classic image of an English narrow-gauge line, Lynton & Barnstaple locomotive 'Taw' hauls its train through the glorious Devon landscape. Opened in 1898, the railway closed in 1935.

CORRIS RAILWAY TRAIN CROSSING THE DOVEY

WORKING ON THE RAILWAY

Railways have always been labour-intensive, and in their heyday hundreds of thousands of men and women were employed across the network. Mechanization, rationalization and extensive closure programmes in the British Railways era led to large numbers being cut, a pattern of staff reduction that has been steadily maintained. However, even today the successful operation and maintenance of the network is dependent upon people. The diversity of tasks undertaken by railway staff and the unusual skills exhibited have always attracted both the casual spectator and the amateur photographer. The legacy of the latter is a huge unofficial and often under-appreciated archive, documenting railwaymen and women at work, from the ever-popular drivers and stationmasters to porters, shunters, station staff and maintenance gangs. It is also a curious characteristic of railway employees that they were generally happy to pose for the camera, a reflection of a sense of pride in the job. These old photographs are not hard to find though, sadly, both subject and photographer are generally unnamed. There is no better way to see and enjoy railway history.

▼ A wonderfully evocative railway group poses happily for an unknown photographer. Location too is unknown, as is the date (probably 1930s).

▶ Two unknown men, perhaps driver and fireman, or engineer and enthusiast, pose alongside a locomotive, possibly on shed and probably in the early 1960s.

◄ The cycle of track maintenance, repair and replacement is never-ending. Here, somewhere in Britain in the 1930s, a gang is laying prefabricated track sections. All we know is that 'the chap in the centre is Charlie'.

◄ Bath Green Park's senior driver in 1961 was Dick Every, photographed here in cheery mood on the footplate of the 9.53am train to Bournemouth, somewhere near Chilcompton.

▼ 'Even the railway lines are being relaid at Wilbraham Road station in anticipation of traffic during Royal Show week.' So says the caption on this photograph. Wilbraham Road was south of Manchester and the date is probably the 1930s.

◀ Two men looking suspiciously like enthusiasts hitch a ride on a brake van during shunting operations at Paddington, probably in the early 1960s – a scene unimaginable today. First, this type of shunting is extinct, particularly in a station, and secondly there is now something called Health and Safety.

▼ Railway paperwork was interminable, with everything having to be recorded by hand. Typical were details of wagon movements and contents, wagon condition reports, and much else to do with the movement of freight.

LONDON MIDLAND AND SCOTTISH RAILWAY COMPANY

SHUNTING HORN CODE.

Miles Platting, New Allen Street.

The following is the authorised Code, and no other must be used:—

Up Main to No. 1 Siding	1 Short 1 Long
No. 1 Siding to Up Main	1 Short 1 Crow
Up Main to No. 2 Siding	2 Short 1 Long
No. 2 Siding to Up Main	2 Short 1 Crow
Up Main to Nos. 3, 4, and 5 Sidings	3 Short 1 Long
Nos. 3, 4, and 5 Sidings to Up Main	3 Short 1 Crow
Up East Goods for Shunting	1 Long 1 Short
" " Right Away	1 Long 1 Crow
To or from Turntable	2 Crows 1 Short
" " Up to Down Main	4 Short 1 Long
Down East Goods to Arrival Loop	4 Short 1 Crow
Up East Goods to Brewery High Level	1 Crow 2 Short
Arrival Loop to Brewery High Level	1 Crow 3 Short
From West Up Goods for Shunting	2 Long 1 Short
" " " Right Away	2 Long 1 Crow

The Shunting Horns must only be used for communicating to Signalmen, and not for communicating to Drivers, or for any other purpose.

BY ORDER
of the
CHIEF GENERAL SUPERINTENDENT.

September, 1929.

▲ Railway operations were strictly controlled by the rule book, and the complexity of those rules is perennially fascinating. This is the 1929 authorized LMS 'Shunting Horn Code' for Miles Platting, near Manchester, famous for the Lancashire & Yorkshire Railway's locomotive works. 'No other must be used.'

▶ In April 1935 driver Robert Thomson, his fireman and the guard pose proudly at Haymarket station with their charge, 1921-built former North British locomotive 'The Lord Provost', now smart in LNER colours.

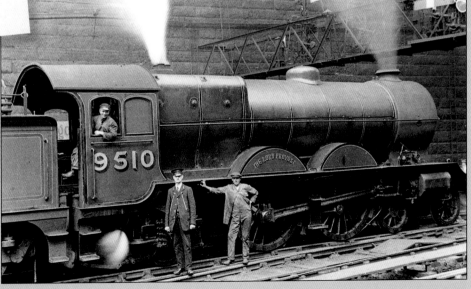

PRIVATE-OWNER WAGONS

P rivately owned wagons have always been
a feature of railways in Britain, although in
the very early days they were regarded with disfavour
by some companies. The North Staffordshire, for
example, refused to allow them on their networks.
Problems arose because of differing manufacturing
standards and specifications, and inadequate
maintenance was held responsible for a number
of accidents. Some of the larger companies, such
as the Midland, tried to buy up privately owned
wagons but in 1914 there were still about 4,000
owners with wagons in use across the network.
The majority were in the coal and mineral trades;
others were built to carry chemicals, cement, gas, oil
and petroleum products, milk, biscuits, mustard, bananas
and even sausages. Today privately owned wagons are
still widely used, for minerals, cement, oil and petrol,
cars and many other products, but tend to be run
as complete trains rather than individually. What
has been lost is the wonderful diversity and the
quirky individuality that added so much interest
to goods trains and goods yards in the pre-British
Railways era.

▲ The coal trade was the primary user of the private-owner wagon and
hundreds of collieries and coal merchants had their names carried all over
Britain on the sides of the standard planked, open wagon. This example is
from Dennyloanhead, west of Falkirk.

▲ Tank wagons were the next most common type after the planked open
wagon. Many were specially built for the oil, gas and petroleum trades. By this
time, the rigid steel chassis and the running gear had been standarized.

▼ The building of private-owner wagons was a highly
competitive business, and companies often photographed
or displayed newly completed vehicles for publicity
purposes. This example belonged to the Birley coal company,
whose collieries were near Sheffield.

▼ The steel industry generally required steel-
built wagons, for durability and safety. At this
point, such wagons had only hand brakes, for
use from ground level, and train braking was
down to the guard's van and the locomotive.

▲ Most private-owner wagons were fairly basic, but luxury vehicles designed for high-speed running did exist, particularly for the food industry. Typical is this 1930s six-wheeled wagon for Palethorpes sausages, built to run on the LMS network.

▲ This is a Welsh example of the typical wooden-bodied, open coal wagon, in this case owned by a coal merchant rather than a colliery.

▼ Proudly displayed by its builder, this high-sided, open wagon was the first to be completed for the Ipswich Gas Company. It would have been used for transporting coal and coke to and from the gas works. Despite this mundane local use, the vehicle shows the careful painting and finishing typical of the private-owner wagon.

▲ Private-owner box vans were less common. Leith General Warehousing had a fleet of these distinctive apex-roofed, wooden vehicles for general cargo distribution.

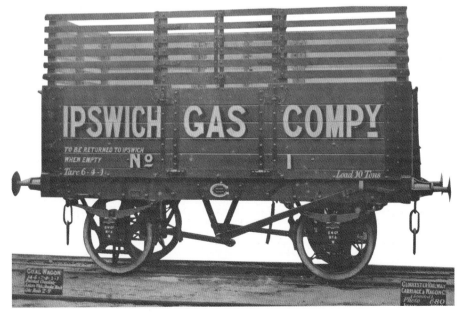

INDUSTRIAL LINES

Industrial railways were in use in Britain during the 17th century. Indeed, the early history of railways is entirely industrial. Primitive wagons were moved by hand or by horsepower on wooden, stone or cast-iron tramways through much of the 18th and early 19th centuries, serving collieries, quarries and iron works. Gauges and sizes varied hugely, from under 2ft to 7ft. Such railways were limited in scale and generally isolated. It was not until a national railway network began to emerge that there was any attempt at standardization or any need to construct sidings that could connect with standard-gauge lines. The earliest steam locomotives, by Trevithick, Blenkinsop and George Stephenson, were built for industrial use. These were followed by a hotchpotch of secondhand and one-off engines that became the mainstay of industrial lines for decades. It was not until the 1860s that manufacturers such as Manning Wardle began to produce ranges of small locomotives specifically for industrial railways, and production in one form or another has continued to the present day.

▼ Coal was the major user of industrial railways, usually standard-gauge, and scenes like this were common until the 1970s. Here, in 1965, an ancient Peckett of 1898 was still in use at Alfreton colliery in Derbyshire.

▼ Many systems were self-contained but others were linked to the main line, with industrial locomotives being used to take wagons to and from the factory sidings.

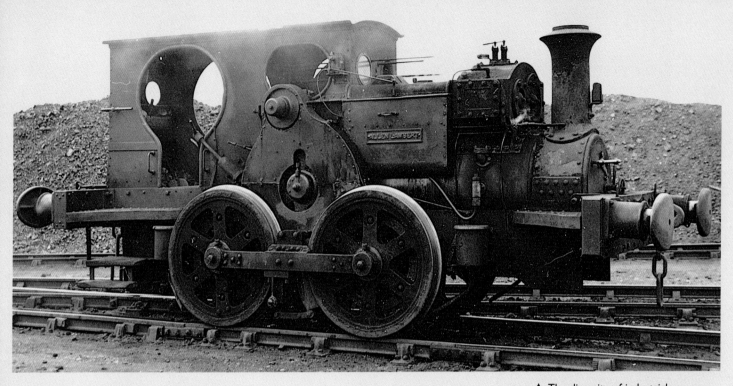

▲ The diversity of industrial locomotives was extraordinary, with many apparently bearing the stamp of Heath Robinson. This eccentric chain-driven example carries a nameplate, 'Allen Lambert', a common practice with such locomotives and reflective of the pride of their operators and their frequent longevity in service.

◄ Neilsons of Glasgow were a major locomotive builder and this inelegant, slab-like vehicle is one of theirs. It was built in 1862 and, judging by the look of its crew, was still at work some forty years later.

► Some industrial locomotives were clearly descended from traction engines and road rollers and some makers, such as Aveling Barford, did produce both. This typically hybrid example was owned by the Cement Marketing Board – hence its name, 'The Blue Circle'.

The diversity of industrial railways in regard to their locomotives, rolling stock and fields of activity was always part of their appeal. Coal was the major user, but to that could be added quarries for stone, slate, sand, clay, iron ore and gravel, as well as brick works, chemical works, breweries, shipyards, docks and corporate activities such as gas and water works, power-generating plants and industrial estates. There was considerable use in agriculture and forestry, particularly for the bulk transport of sugar beet, potatoes and peat. Contractors have always used industrial railways on construction projects, many of which were by definition short-lived, so some manufacturers produced easily transportable vehicles and track designed for temporary use. Associated with these was the development of locomotives driven by petrol or diesel engines. In some cases contractors who built early railways ended up running them themselves, using whatever locomotives and rolling stock could be found. However, passenger-carrying was never a real concern, though some lines had carriages suitable for transporting people to and from work. Industrial lines have declined massively since the 1960s, but a recent example was the extensive network, with over a hundred locomotives, used for some years during the building of the Channel Tunnel.

▲ Quarry locomotives by Manning Wardle, Hawthorn and others were built for use on irregular and often temporary narrow-gauge track, usually 3ft or less. These three, long out of use, await the cutter's torch.

▲ Looking smart, despite its age, and posing proudly with its crew, 'Covertcoat' is a typical Leeds-built quarry locomotive of 1898. A rare survivor, this now has a very different life on the Launceston Railway.

◄ Many locomotives have carried the name 'Nelson'. This example was owned by Cardiff Corporation and was used in the docks. Judging by the small boy, the photograph dates from the 1920s.

▲ This smartly turned-out Andrew Barclay 0-4-0 worked at one of ICI's chemical plants. Industrial locomotives were often very well cared for and many enjoyed a long life, with one or a number of owners.

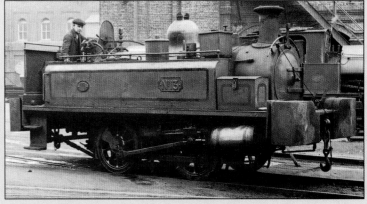

▲ Many gas works had narrow-gauge railways which often featured low-profile locomotives designed to move easily among the retort sheds. No. 13 is seen here at work at Beckton, in east London, in 1954.

◄ The combined challenge of road transport and industrial decline was too much for many industrial railways and from the 1960s thousands of locomotives went to the scrapyard.

▲ This Andrew Barclay saddle tank locomotive was no. 1 in the fleet operated by the Central Electricity Authority (London Division). Power stations were coal-fired, so locomotives such as this were constantly at work moving lines of coal wagons to and from the main line.

◄ Some industrial locomotives enjoyed a remarkably long life. This Hawthorn 0-4-0 was approaching its centenary when photographed still in use in 1950 at a pottery works. Clay and industrial ceramics businesses, such as brick and pipe works, were major users of industrial railways.

NORTHERN
ENGLAND

LOST & FOUND

▲ A WILD GROWTH of nature has completely hidden the trackbed, but a bridge, near Kettleness in Yorkshire, survives to show that there once was a railway from Whitby to Redcar.

► MOST CLOSED STATIONS vanished, but some gained a new life as houses, while retaining their definable station style of architecture. This is Lartington, near Barnard Castle, Durham.

▼ NOTHING IS MORE EVOCATIVE of a long-lost railway than a handsome tunnel. Many survive, but are generally inaccessible and thus full of mystery, and bats. This is near Burdale, on the old Malton-to-Driffield line.

DERWENT VALLEY LIGHT RAILWAY

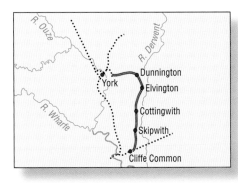

The Light Railways Act of 1896 inspired many minor railways, the majority of which were rural or local branch lines aimed primarily at passenger traffic. Something rather different was the Derwent Valley Light Railway, whose 16-mile route from Layerthorpe, in York, to Cliffe Common, near Selby, was built between 1911 and 1913. Conceived largely as a freight line, it nevertheless had eleven stations, most of which were built in an appealing cricket-pavilion style. Its passenger services were operated by rudimentary railbuses. With connections at both ends and a meandering route that paralleled at a distance the direct line from York to Selby via Naburn, it had a certain diversionary value, and was used in this way by the NER during World War I. Despite this, it had little appeal to the larger companies that surrounded it and so remained independent.

The DVLR managed to escape the Grouping of 1923 and, even more unusually, nationalization, and it never came under the control of British Railways. By then passenger services had long gone, having ceased on 1 September 1926, but there was enough freight (mostly agricultural – hence the DVLR was affectionately known as the Farmers' Line) to keep the railway open, and firmly in private hands, until the 1960s. In World War II it again proved its value as a diversionary route, but more important was its role in transporting bombs to the big RAF Bomber

▲ On the outskirts of York, near Tang Hall, an old bridge over the former trackbed has been decorated with sculpture by Sustrans and with graffiti by local residents.

▼ The DVLR shed at York Layerthorpe, a ramshackle affair, was indicative of the somewhat primitive nature of much of the railway.

▼ This is the menu and toast list used at a DVLR celebration dinner to mark the coronation of King George V in 1911. The diversity of toasts indicates the general spirit of optimism of that era.

Menu.

SOUPS.

Oxtail.   Tomato.

FISH.

Boiled Cod   Shrimp Sauce.

JOINTS.

Roast Beef.   Horseradish Sauce.

Boiled Mutton.   Caper Sauce.

SWEETS.

Plum Pudding   Rum Sauce.

Cheese and Biscuits.

Celery.

Toast List.

"THE KING."

"THE DIRECTORS."
Proposer : Mr. S. J. Reading.
Responder : Mr. C. W. Thompson.

"SUCCESS TO THE D.V.L.R."
Proposer : Mr. L. Foster.
Responder : Major H. A. Watson, C.B.E.,
[M.V.O.

"DONORS AND VISITORS."
Proposer : Mr. H. J. Silke.
Responder : Mr. T. J. Vellacott
[Messrs. Shell-Mex Ltd.).

"D.V. EMPLOYEES' SOCIAL CLUB."
Proposer : Mr. F. Cartledge.
Responder : Mr. W. J. Privett.

"HOST AND HOSTESS."
Proposer : Mr. J. A. Ratlidge.

ENTERTAINMENT.
The following Artistes will entertain—
Messrs. Bob Machin, A. W. Gell,
P. Laycock.
Accompanied by Mr. A. Smith.

"God Save the King."

▲ Murton Park station (formerly Wheldrake but rebuilt on its present site) is the headquarters of the Derwent Valley Light Railway preservation society. This shows the characteristic cricket pavilion-cum-bungalow style favoured by the DVLR in 1913 for its stations.

▼ Freight trains continued to operate throughout the railway's life. Locomotives were ancient and the wagons were varied, adding to the character of this private railway. Here, a typical train passes Dunnington Halt.

Command airfield at Elvington (now the Yorkshire Air Museum). It was said that the line's overgrown nature made it naturally camouflaged.

In 1964 British Railways closed the line from Selby to Hull, and the Derwent Valley's southern mainline link turned into a branch line. A year later the southern section, from Cliffe to Wheldrake, was closed, and then progressive closures took place up to 1973, by which time only the 4 miles from Dunnington to Layerthorpe remained open. Between 1977 and 1979 the railway's private owners operated regular steam services during the summer to attract tourists, and limited freight trains continued to run until 1981, at which point closure brought the story to an end. The remaining track was lifted soon after.

Today, despite its relatively recent demise, much of the route has gone. The northern section, from Layerthorpe to Osbaldwick, is part of a Sustrans cycle route. The next station, Murton Park, is the headquarters of the Derwent Valley Light Railway, a preservation society with a collection of locomotives and rolling stock, a fully restored DVLR station and a short length of track. South from here there is little to see, with the trackbed returned to the fields from which it came. Near Wheldrake are old warehouses and loading bays formerly linked to the railway. Skipwith station has been fully restored as a private house, complete with two carriages, while at the site of Cliffe Common there is an old platform and beyond it the grand junction station, also now a private dwelling.

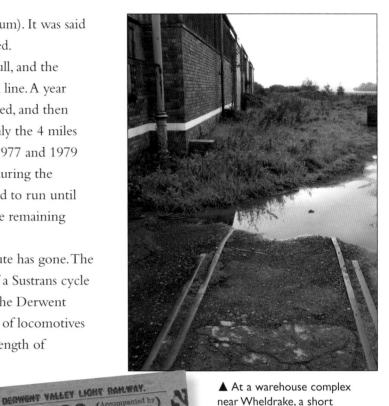

▲ At a warehouse complex near Wheldrake, a short stretch of track survives in the tarmac, a reminder of the line's dependence upon goods traffic.

DERWENT VALLEY LIGHT RAILWAY.
ONE DOG (Accompanied by Passenger)
At Co's Ltd. risk rate. See conditions on back.
YORK (Layerthorpe) to
For one journey under 10 miles. This ticket is available for a single journey only.
Must be given up at destination station.
FARE 6d.

▼ Skipwith station has been delightfully restored. The two carriages adjoining it are used for holiday letting.

▲ Cliffe Common was the southern end of the DVLR, where it met the Selby-to-Hull line. All has gone save the big old station, which is now a private house, and a surviving section of overgrown platform.

▼ This distant view of Thorganby station, near the southern end of the line, was taken soon after it was opened. Passenger services were still operating (they finished in 1926) and the station buildings give a good sense of the economical nature of the line's structures.

COCKERMOUTH TO SELLAFIELD

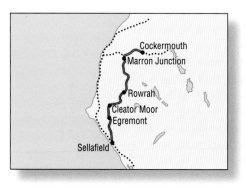

One of Britain's best railway journeys today is along the Cumbrian coast from Carlisle to Barrow, with its spectacular section from Maryport to Ravenglass virtually on the beach, overshadowed by hills and cliffs. This line, the only one in this part of England, fights for survival physically and economically. Though isolated today, it was once the backbone of an extensive network spreading inland and linking remote places. Minerals were the inspiration, the lines making accessible huge deposits of iron ore and, later, haematite. The start, in the 1840s, was the Maryport & Carlisle Railway; others soon followed. The Whitehaven & Furness Junction built much of the coastal route, and the 1860s saw the completion of the route eastwards across the Lake District to Penrith, most of which was built by the Cockermouth, Keswick & Penrith Railway.

The development of this route, from Cockermouth south to the coast at Sellafield, was more fragmented. Things started in the south, with the opening in 1857 of the Whitehaven, Cleator & Egremont Railway. This had a slow start but as the mineral traffic developed it became very busy. Other local companies, such as the Cleator & Workington Junction, completed the network by the 1870s, with much of it eventually coming under the control of the ambitious Furness Railway. The ever-increasing importance of mineral traffic also inspired the building of some independent branches, such as the Rowrah & Kelton Fell Railway. However,

▼ Cockermouth's station has disappeared but, as this Edwardian photograph indicates, it was a substantial building reflecting various periods of expansion. As ever in photographs from this era, the people awaiting the train are all remarkably well dressed.

► Between Ashby and Ullock the route of the railway can be seen as a low embankment running across the landscape against a magnificent backdrop of Lakeland hills.

▼ It is a sunny day in about 1910 and all seems well with the world as Bridgefoot's stationmaster and a small boy pose for the camera. At this point passengers were still important on the route, but it was the mineral traffic that created the revenue.

iron and haematite boom came to an end after World War I, so the lines began to close. The Rowrah branch had gone by 1927 and passenger traffic on the southern section ended in 1935. Closures were progressive from this point, and it all came to an end in 1966, when Cockermouth itself vanished from the network.

Despite these closures being relatively early, there is still plenty for the explorer to find. From Cockermouth south to Bridgefoot, roads have obliterated everything, but from here the route along the valley of the river Marron can be traced, with the section from Ullock to Wright Green being a footpath, offering wonderful views eastwards towards the Lake District. A low embankment that carried the line to Rowrah is still visible. Four lines met at Rowrah, and there is much still to be seen, though working it all out is rather complicated. The trackbed can then be traced to Cleator, with bridges and a station (now a private house) still in situ. The Sustrans Coast-2-Coast footpath crosses near Moor End. South of Cleator things are not so clear. A new bypass near Egremont has buried quite a bit but at Egremont the last link with the iron industry that for so long was the economic backbone of the region is to be found in Florence Mine, the deepest iron ore mine in Europe and still working, though no longer rail-connected. From here south to Thornhill the trackbed becomes an official footpath and cycleway, and then it remains visible as an embankment south of Beckermet, where there was another iron ore branch. At Sellafield, in the shadow of the huge nuclear installation, the Cumbrian coast line brings back a railway reality.

▼ Lines around Rowrah closed progressively from the late 1920s but some track was still in place in the 1960s. Here, the demolition gang is removing the last remains of what had been an extensive local network.

▲ When lines disappear bridges carrying footpaths usually go as well, because they are no longer necessary. This elegant iron footbridge spanning the overgrown trackbed to the west of Cleator is, therefore, an unexpected survivor and a considerable rarity.

▼ Though no longer rail-connected (ridiculous though that seems), Egremont's massive Florence iron ore mine is still in operation. The old buildings give a hint of what the region must have been like when it was one of Britain's major iron ore and haematite producers.

LOST STATIONS: NORTHERN ENGLAND

Railways were born in the north of England, so it is no surprise that the region was served by a remarkable density of lines. The inspiration was industry, mining, iron and steel, ship building, textiles, ports and harbours, engineering and chemicals, and the tough landscape was merely a challenge to be overcome as railways crossed the Pennines and penetrated the Lake District, despite the protestations of poet and local resident William Wordsworth. From the early days, rival companies fought bitterly over the territory and great fortunes were made and lost. The network spread rapidly, linking the great cities, towns and centres of industry with remote country regions, hitherto little known and inaccessible. Where industry led, tourism soon followed, and railways opened up the landscape, lakes, rivers and coasts of Yorkshire, Lancashire, Cumbria and Northumberland, turning traditional and famous towns and unknown villages into thriving resorts. Main lines formed a grid across the region, but in between were hundreds of miles of lesser lines and branches, connecting countless stations. The diversity was remarkable, from the great temples to the railway age, represented by York, Leeds and Manchester, to tiny halts on isolated branch lines. There was much duplication of both routes and stations, so closures were inevitable. In fact, some of the earliest closures in Britain took place in the heartlands of railway history. However, the major losses came in the 1960s and early 1970s as the North suffered particularly because of that same density of network that had in the past been a symbol of wealth and success. Here is a small and random selection of some of those lost stations.

▼ An early closure, in 1930, was the line that wandered across the wilds of Northumbria from Alnwick to Coldstream. Kirknewton was one of ten intermediate stations. More than sixty-five years on, it was still recognizably a station, despite the vehicles on the trackbed.

▼ Southport was remarkably well equipped with stations, having at one time nine with the town's name in the title. It was, after all, a resort created by the railways. Today, there is one station. This photograph shows Southport Chapel Street, a typical piece of Victorian classicism, in 1971, near the end of its life.

▶ Passengers and the stationmaster pose for the camera in front of Sinnington's fine stone station, probably in the 1920s. The station, and the line from Pickering to Pilmoor Junction, closed in 1953.

▼ One of the last closures in the region, in 1972, was the line to Keswick from Penrith. One of the stations along the line was Blencow, seen here on the last day of service, 4 February. A solitary traveller huddles against the cold.

▼ An ambulance and a family with a baby in an old-fashioned pram wait and watch as a double-headed enthusiasts' special passes through Stanley, near Methley, east of Leeds, in 1958.

LOST JOURNEY: WHITEHAVEN TO WHITBY

With most main lines running south to north, crossing the country from west to east was always a slow and cumbersome process, particularly in the north of England. The most direct route, Carlisle to Newcastle, was too far north for this journey, while the cross-Pennine routes radiating from Manchester were too far south. On the map, the journey is almost a straight line, but the reality is very different. There were four changes and a couple of bad connections, resulting in long waits at unpromising locations. The total travelling time is nearly 12 hours. However, there were compensations, with views over some of the best landscape in England. The first part of the journey is through the Lake District on the only line that crossed the spectacular region, to poet William Wordsworth's disgust. Then comes the crossing of the Pennines, with the heights of Stainmore, and the descent through Barnard Castle to Darlington, birthplace of the railways. The final section is across the North Yorkshire Moors and along river valleys to Whitby. It is a coast-to-coast journey from one scenic harbour to another. Today, the journey is impossible: all has gone except the final stretch into Whitby.

TIMETABLE

Whitehaven.............................	5.55am
Workington.............................	6.16am
Change	
Workington.............................	6.45am
Penrith.....................................	8.37am
Change	
Penrith.....................................	10.14am
Darlington...............................	1.01pm
Change	
Darlington...............................	1.30pm
Eaglescliffe Junction..........	1.47pm
Change	
Eaglescliffe Junction..........	3.56pm
Whitby Town.......................	6.15pm

PENRITH
WORKINGTON
Keswick
Appleby
WHITEHAVEN
Kirkby Stephen

► WELL SITED and with a rich history, Whitehaven derived its wealth and status from its extensive harbour. This was at its peak in the Victorian era but continued to flourish well into the 20th century. In this card the quays are empty but the extensive network of quayside railways is hard at work.

THE HARBOUR FROM PROSPECT, WHITEHAVEN
S.756

◄ WITH WELL OVER an hour to wait at Penrith, there would be ample time to explore the handsome red-sandstone, Tudor-style station, then a major junction, and to see the fine church tower and the ruined 14th-century castle. Those feeling energetic could climb Penrith Beacon for views into Scotland – but should not risk missing the train.

► DARLINGTON'S GRAND covered 1880s station is an easy place to spend half an hour waiting for a train. Much of the time could be spent examining George Stephenson's famous 'Locomotion', no.1 of the Stockton & Darlington Railway. Built in 1825, this was on display for many years on the station's concourse beneath the impressive three-arched train shed with its decorative supporting pillars. This station, Bank Top, was Darlington's main station, while North Road, though much earlier, was always less important. However, today North Road is a museum, and those wishing to see 'Locomotion' have to go there.

Engine No. 1, Darlington Station.

◄ A BUSY PLACE where four lines meet, Eaglescliffe Junction was, however, never an ideal spot for a two-hour wait. Only the dedicated train enthusiast could pass the time profitably. There would probably be time for a quick detour to Stockton or Middlesbrough, but missing the connection for the final stage to Whitby could be a disaster.

Barnard Castle DARLINGTON EAGLESCLIFFE WHITBY

► WHITBY HAD LONG been famous as a harbour but its reputation as a resort was entirely due to the railways. The simple classical terminus station right by the harbour was opened in 1847 and then, as now, the view from the station was exactly as depicted on this Edwardian card. Later, another station, Whitby West Cliff, was built high above the town to serve trains on the dramatic coastal route from Scarborough to Redcar. This has gone, along with its line, but GT Andrews's pleasing little masterpiece lives on.

Whitby from the Station.

TURNTABLES

Locomotives, as well as some other vehicles, have, by their nature, always had to be turned, so turntables of one kind or another have been associated with stations, engine sheds and goods yards since the 1830s. Initially quite primitive, these became more sophisticated as locomotives increased in size and weight and, from the 1870s, the standard turntable was set in a pit and balanced on a central pivot, with outer guiding wheels. Initially locomotives were pushed round by their crews, but larger turntables demanded mechanical operation by electricity or via the locomotive's own vacuum braking system. Another turning system used a dedicated triangle of track.

▲ In the summer of 1953 a Southern Region Merchant Navy class locomotive no. 35026, 'Lamport & Holt Line', is slowly driven from the remarkably overgrown siding on to the turntable at Folkestone. Meanwhile, crew and some shed staff take a breather.

▼ By 1936, when this photograph was taken, turntables were often mechanically operated. However, at many places the application of manpower was still the only way to turn a locomotive. Here, at York, the crew struggle to turn no. 5093, a new-looking Stanier Black 5.

► Every terminus station of significance had to have a turntable. This is Kingswear, Devon, in November 1935, as GWR King class no. 6014 'King Henry VII' is slowly turned by hand. The locomotive is carrying its short-lived and rather ungainly streamlining.

▼ In May 1966 the steam age is nearing its end and turntable use is becoming a bit of a novelty. Spectators have gathered at Salisbury to watch Southern U class no. 31639 being turned after working an enthusiasts' special.

THE RAILWAY EXECUTIVE.
B.R. 32709/5.

NOTICE.

LOCOMOTIVE TURNTABLES.

Drivers must be careful to run steadily on to a turntable in order to obviate the necessity for applying the brakes suddenly as this is liable to damage the turntable and particularly the centre bearing.

The locking levers must not be thrown over before the turntable is at rest after turning.

The plungers at both ends of the turntable must be in position in the shoes before a locomotive is moved on to or off the turntable, and the locking levers secured by the safety pins, where provided.

Locomotives must be stopped about 6 feet from the turntable before moving on it to turn.

It must be distinctly understood that when the table is being manually operated by levers the table must be **pushed** and not **pulled** round.

MOTIVE POWER SUPERINTENDENT.

▲ The alternative to a turntable was a dedicated triangle of track. This one is at Woodford Halse, on the Great Central line, in 1963, with a good crop of dandelions in flower. Today, few turntables survive in use, so preserved locomotives on mainline specials use triangles or run tender-first.

GOODS TRAINS

From the very early days railways were built to carry goods, or freight, and this set a pattern that dominated the structure and principles of the railway system in Britain throughout the 19th century and well into the 20th. The carrying of passengers, initially seen as unimportant or incidental, did begin to dominate railway planning in the 1840s and 1850s and indeed during these decades passenger revenue exceeded the income from goods. From that point the balance shifted, and until the mid-1960s goods revenues were always greater. This was due to a number of factors, including the creation of efficient and nationwide distribution networks, the construction of specialized wagons, the centralization of revenue-gathering via the Railway Clearing House, the development of national parcels services and the improved handling facilities for bulk cargoes. Also significant in the 20th century was the steady integration of road and rail transport systems, to ensure point-to-point collection and delivery, and the use of various kinds of container to simplify cargo handling.

During the Victorian period many railway fortunes were made, and in some cases subsequently lost, through the great expansion of goods traffic.

▲ In a scene familiar for over a century, a British Railways classic from the last phase of steam, a class 9F 2-10-0 heavy freight locomotive, no. 92025 of 1955, one of only ten fitted with a Franco-Crosti boiler, hauls a long mixed-goods train across the flat Midlands landscape near Braunston, in 1964.

▼ With the steam age coming to an end, even the most famous locomotives could find themselves hauling freight trains. In August 1965, a Gresley streamlined A4 Pacific, no. 60027, 'Merlin', makes light work of a cement train near Lunan Bay, south of Montrose.

▲ In the summer of 1959 a narrow-profile diesel multiple unit built for the Hastings line overtakes a mixed-goods train near Orpington while the driver of the old Southern Railway N class locomotive, no. 31873, looks on.

▼ The double-headed goods train was always a splendid sight. In the last years of steam some unusual pairings could sometimes be seen, such as an LMS Black 5 and a British Railways 9F, captured here in 1967 fighting the heavy gradients of the Borders with a Whitehaven-to-Gartsherrie goods.

Notably successful was the carriage of coal, at a time when the country's industrial, commercial and domestic life was entirely dependent upon coal. At this time coal was also exported in prodigious quantities. This pattern was to continue until the early 1950s, when 70 per cent of coal traffic in Britain still went by train. The result of all this was that goods trains and goods traffic were a familiar feature on practically every line in Britain, great and small. Most stations had goods yards and good sheds, and even the smallest had some form of freight or parcels handling facility. In addition, there were many lines, stations and depots built specifically for goods traffic. The majority of railway companies had fleets of goods locomotives, although the realities of railway operation on a day-to-day basis meant that there was a regular crossover between goods and passenger services.

There were many kinds of goods trains, from the major long-distance services, running to regular schedules, to little local pick-up freights, collecting the occasional wagon from rural backwaters. However, the most familiar was the mixed freight, a long line of assorted wagons assembled in large marshalling yards and headed by one or two locomotives. Such trains were a regular sight on any railway journey, either rumbling through stations or waiting in sidings and passing loops. Shunting, the process of sorting wagons in major freight yards or rural sidings, was also an integral part of any railway experience,

▲ The mixed freight lived on well into the 1970s and the diesel era. Here, in 1973, assorted wagons topped and tailed by brake vans are hauled past the old Peak Forest station, in Derbyshire, by a class 40 diesel.

▼ The urban goods train was an important part of the story, even in electrified commuter land. Against the background of a busy yard, a Metropolitan tank hauls a train of empty coal wagons off the Uxbridge branch in the 1930s.

◀ Two elderly locomotives, a fifty-year-old class C and a younger U1, work together in an unconventional manner with a small mixed-goods near Edenbridge, Kent, in 1960, in a typically rural setting.

1005/11 1,000 2/42

CHESHIRE LINES. 186

URGENT--Perishables

Date .... 194...

From Birkenhead (Shore Road Station)

To _____

Via Helsby & Godley

TOTAL NUMBER OF SHEETS

IN or ON Wagon _____

Owner and No. of Wagon _____

Consignee _____

3

▼ With a classic mix of box vans and open wagons, a slightly battered Hymek locomotive, D7074, keeps the traditional goods train alive near Frome, Somerset, in 1964.

and very familiar to anyone old enough to remember the 1960s and 1970s. The diversity of goods trains, and everything to do with them, was part of their appeal. The modern freight train, usually composed of containers or bulk cargoes such as stone, coal, cement, oil products or new cars, simply cannot compete in terms of character or excitement.

What has also disappeared is the brake van. Until the 1970s every goods train, however large or small, had to have a brake van, a practice that went back to the 1850s. The brake van was usually a box-like vehicle on four wheels, sometimes with an open verandah, and with minimal facilities, such as a stove for the guard, who was in charge of the train. Until the mid-20th century goods wagons often had no linked braking system, so the control of the train was dependent upon the locomotive and the guard's handbrake in the brake van. Vacuum braking systems for goods trains were introduced gradually from the 1920s but, even after these were in regular use, the brake van remained an essential part of any goods train. Brake vans varied from company to company but basically they were heavy vehicles, to increase their braking power, and the general design principles remained consistent until the last ones were built in the 1960s. By the 1980s, unbraked or partially braked goods trains had disappeared and this, combined with the introduction of single-manned or driver-controlled trains, brought the brake van to its end. At the same time, the traditional goods train, a vital component of the railway scene for 150 years, also disappeared from the network.

▲ Steam is in its last year, yet the timeless process of shunting continues. In 1967, amid overgrown sidings at Kirkby Stephen East, a class 4MT locomotive, no. 43049, takes its time while collecting a single open wagon.

▼ In a glorious Cumbrian setting near Lowca in 1968, a Type 1 diesel runs a single brake van along a freight line north of Whitehaven.

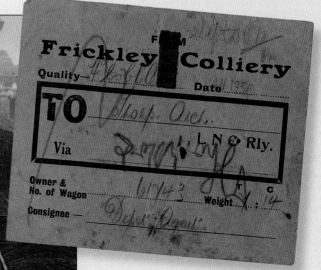

Frickley Colliery

Quality _____ Date _____

TO _____
Via _____ L N E Rly.

Owner &
No. of Wagon _____ Weight _____
Consignee _____

◄ When coal was king, Ashington was the unofficial capital of the Northumberland coalfield and in the days of steam it was a scene of continuous activity as the local tank engines unceasingly shunted the lines of coal wagons. In this smoky and grimy setting, an old class J27 winds its way through the colliery yards, hauling a loaded coal train to Blyth, for onward shipment. The dependence of the coal industry upon the railways, and coal's dominant position for so long at the heart of goods traffic, is captured by this scene.

► By 1961 the old Devon line from Heathfield to Exeter was no longer in use north of Trusham, yet the long-closed station still received its thrice-weekly pick-up goods. On 10 August GWR pannier tank locomotive no. 3659 had to be content with a couple of bulk cement wagons.

WAGONS AT REST

The gradual reduction of railway goods traffic from the 1950s resulted in many thousands of goods vehicles being made redundant. Some were stored in long lines on remote sidings and left to decay quietly, while others were broken up for scrap, though this was rarely worth the effort. However, it had long been appreciated that some railway vehicles, notably box vans, make excellent sheds, so wagon bodies were sold off in huge numbers, mainly to farmers to serve as stores and animal shelters. As a result, the countryside of Britain is littered with the remains of vast numbers of former goods wagons, most now nearing the end of their life.

▲ This 'old railway vehicle', as the caption describes it, was photographed in the 1930s on a farm near Hooe. Clearly on its last legs then, this Victorian vehicle shows how long-established the reuse habit was. Hooe never had a station but nearby Battle did, and still does.

▲ Brynammon was once the meeting point of the Midland and the Great Western in the dense network of colliery lines north of Swansea. Mines and railways have now vanished into history, but traces remain. This former wooden box van, having enjoyed a new life as a dwelling, was photographed in 1991.

▶ The island of Arran, off the west coast of Scotland, never had an inch of railway line, yet former railway vehicles still made their way there, such was their value to farmers. Photographed in 2006, this now abandoned feed store or animal shelter still reveals its railway origins.

► When lines close, everything that can be moved is usually taken away, generally for scrap. However, sometimes unexpected things get left behind: these tank vehicles were found quietly rotting away in woods near Llanilar, on the old line south of Aberystwyth.

▼ In the 1990s, woods near Gainford, west of Darlington, concealed several former vehicles. Traces of paintwork on this metal box van reveal that it was condemned in the 1960s.

RAILWAY SHIPS

B etween the 1840s and 1984 railways and shipping were closely connected. More than fifty railway companies owned or operated many hundreds of ships during that period, from Lake District and Clyde pleasure steamers and cross-Channel ferries to cargo vessels, dredgers and tugs. Railway companies also built or controlled ports and harbours all round the coast of Britain, and from these they operated scheduled passenger and freight services to Ireland, the Channel Islands, France and Belgium, Germany and the Netherlands, and Scandinavia. The first railway-controlled shipping services were over the river Hull, across the Irish Sea from Holyhead, and over the Channel to France and the Channel Islands. The network grew rapidly as more railway companies started more and more services, often in direct competition with each other. As ever, the railways were conscious of their image as well as their territory, so ships carried clear railway company branding. The competitive nature of the business was underlined by stylish posters and publicity material.

Particular types of ships also appeared. They were usually fast day

▶ SS *Scotia* was a LNWR ship on the Holyhead-to-Dublin service in the Edwardian era. This card was used to promote all LNWR services to Ireland via Holyhead on their 'magnificent steamers'. It gave journey times from Euston, for example to Galway, 14 hours.

L.&N.W.S.S. SCOTIA LEAVING HOLYHEAD FOR DUBLIN (NORTH WALL)

B.D. No. 30150 Ex.

ONE-DAY EXCURSION TICKET

Folkestone to Boulogne

No Luggage allowed.

1st CLASS. | Available by the Boats as advertised.

IMPORTANT NOTICE.

This Ticket may be used without a Passport only by a British subject, or by a French or Belgian subject who is resident in the United Kingdom. Any other person using this Ticket must be in possession of a valid Passport.

The holder must fill up, in ink or indelible pencil, pages 1, 3, 4 and 6 before embarkation. Separate Embarkation and Landing Identity Cards are not required, but the ordinary Landing Card of the Railway Company, issued on board in exchange for the Boat Coupon, must still be given up at the gangway.

A French or Belgian subject must produce his British Identity Book or Registration Certificate with this Ticket to the Immigration Officer on return to Folkestone, otherwise leave to land may be refused (voir au dos).

FOR CONDITIONS ON WHICH THESE COUPONS ARE ISSUED SEE END OF TICKET.

Date of Issue

Printed by McCorquodale & Co. Ltd., London.

L.&N.W. S.S. "SCOTIA" SMOKING CABIN
HOLYHEAD & DUBLIN SERVICE

▲ There was always plenty of free promotional material. This 1960s lapel badge was issued by British and French Railways car ferries.

◀ This view of the *Scotia*'s smoking cabin shows the standard of decor in railway ferries before World War I.

224

◄ Day trips across the Channel were always popular and for many of them passports were not necessary. This first-class Folkestone-to-Boulogne ticket was issued by the Southern Railway to Ronald Cross in June 1926. This was valid only on the 10.15am boat, so it would have been a short day in Boulogne.

► The Glasgow & South Western was one of several Scottish railway companies with shipping interests. This Edwardian card promotes one of their latest vessels on the Clyde routes, the *Atalanta*, a fast, modern turbine ship.

G.& S.W.Ry.Cos
T.S."Atalanta"

◄ Services between Newhaven and Dieppe were operated jointly by British and French railway companies, and this continued until the demise of Sealink in 1984. The *Senlac* was in service in the late 1970s and early 1980s, maintaining the tradition of familiar ships dedicated to the route.

▼ An Edwardian view of the Ladies' Boudoir on the SS *Brighton*, the LB&SCR's latest turbine ship, used on the Newhaven-to-Dieppe run. This promotional card advertises a three-hour crossing. Today's takes four hours.

▲ There were several scheduled train ferry services, mostly from Dover or Harwich. This is a British Railways wagon label used on the Zeebrugge service.

LADIES' BOUDOIR, TURBINE S.S. "BRIGHTON," L.B. & S.C.R.   *Waterlow & Sons Ltd.*

boats, with comfortable passenger facilities, built for rapid journeys and a quick turnaround. Sleeping accommodation was available on longer routes. There were also train ferries and dedicated cargo vessels and, from the 1930s, car carriers, though the first drive-on, drive-off ships did not appear until the 1950s. Joint ventures were common between railway and independent shipping companies and internationally, with some cross-Channel services being operated by French or Belgian and British companies in tandem.

When British Railways came into being in 1948, it took control of all existing railway shipping services and gained the freedom to operate routes wherever and whenever it wanted. A degree of standardization was applied to new ships, but they were still up-to-the-minute and innovative vessels, and most of the pre-war routes continued to operate, along with some new ones. British Rail was an early user of the hovercraft, with its Seaspeed routes in 1966. In 1970 the Sealink brand was launched and applied to all shipping services, even the ancient Windermere pleasure steamers. Railway control of shipping services ended in 1984.

▲ British Railways used stylish graphics to promote connecting services across Europe. This 1960 brochure covers travel to the French and Italian rivieras.

◄ By 1963, when this brochure was produced, most cross-Channel ships were car ferries. This promoted services from Dover, with the cost for a car starting at £3 (single).

▲ This 1955 brochure promoting Channel Islands services has a period quality typical of British Railways.

▼ ► The Golden Arrow was always the style leader in cross-Channel travel. This elegant brochure is from 1959, when the return fare was £16. 8s. Below is a luggage label designed to adorn the smartest suitcases.

▲ Issued by British Rail's PR department in the 1970s, this photograph shows the newly modernized ferry terminal at Fishguard.

▼ From the early days Hull was a major railway port, as this Edwardian NER promotional postcard indicates.

► This 1961 British Railways brochure gives details of the Holyhead-to-Dun Laoghaire services, with connecting trains to London. The ships boasted a Cabin de Luxe for £3 (first-class passengers only).

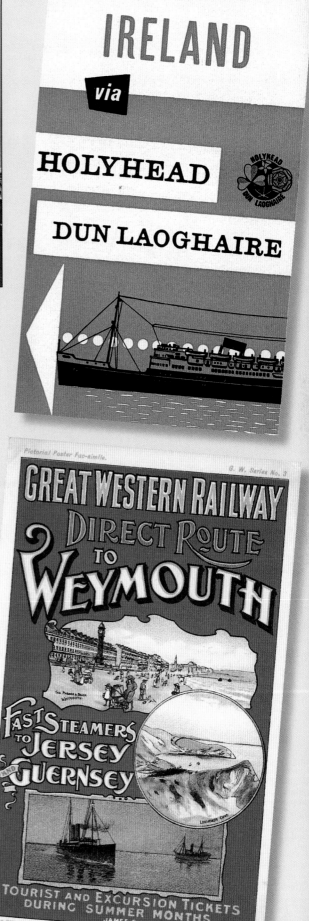

► Although Weymouth was served by both the GWR and the LSWR (and later the SR), the Great Western had control of the Channel Islands shipping services, as this Edwardian advertisement makes clear.

Dining Room

S.S. "ISLE of GUERNSEY"

Gents Lounge.

◀ This Edwardian advertising postcard promotes a new ship on the Channel Islands service and shows its lavish decor.

▶ A 1947 Southern Railway brochure gives details of cross-Channel services for cars, motorcycles and caravan and baggage trailers. At this time, vehicles were still loaded by crane.

Seaspeed

Hovercraft services to

Paris and Brussels

May 2 - October 22 1977

◀ British Rail's Seaspeed cross-Channel hovercraft services were introduced in 1966. In 1977 the sailings were still train-connected, and a single from London to Paris was £17.75.

SOUTHERN RAILWAY
CONVEYANCE
OF
MOTOR CARS,
MOTOR-CYCLES,
CARAVAN & BAGGAGE TRAILERS
TO AND FROM
THE
CONTINENT
AND
CHANNEL ISLANDS

DOVER—CALAIS
FOLKESTONE—CALAIS
FOLKESTONE—BOULOGNE
DOVER—BOULOGNE
NEWHAVEN—DIEPPE
DOVER—OSTEND
SOUTHAMPTON—HAVRE
SOUTHAMPTON—CHANNEL ISLANDS
JERSEY—ST. MALO

SERVICES, RATES & FARES
BY ALL ROUTES

SUMMER—1947

Waterloo Station, S.E.1.

Ctl./50 10 46200
25/6/47

E. J. MISSENDEN,
General Manager.

Printed in Great Britain by
M'Corquodale & Co. Ltd., London.

▼ Ferry and pleasure steamer routes around the Clyde and the Scottish islands were very competitive, and a number of railways ran fleets of ships, including the Caledonian.

CALEDONIAN RAILWAY

CALEDONIAN CLYDE TOURIST STEAMERS

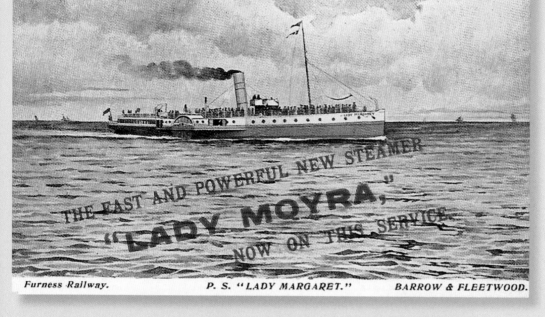

Furness Railway.   P. S. "LADY MARGARET."   BARROW & FLEETWOOD.

◀ The Furness Railway was a small but ambitious railway whose wealth initially came from the exploitation of haematite deposits north of Barrow. Later, it was a pioneer in the development of tourism and became well known for its fleet of fast, modern pleasure steamers. This Edwardian card, published by the Furness itself, promotes their latest ship, the paddle steamer *Lady Moyra*.

◀ ▼ In 1959 the *Maid of Kent*, British Railways' latest and most modern cross-Channel ferry, came into service. Though small by modern standards, the *Maid* was at the time widely regarded as state of the art. These British Railways publicity photographs from May 1959 show the ship, the master's cabin, the restaurant and a cut-away drawing highlighting the two-storey car deck, the buffet and the restaurant.

S.S. MAID OF KENT CROSS CHANNEL CAR FERRY

NAMEPLATES

T he practice of naming locomotives goes back to the dawn of railways, perhaps echoing maritime traditions. However, with the rapid increase in the numbers of locomotives from the 1850s, more definite forms of identification became necessary and many railways were prompted to adopt numbers as well as names. Initially both were applied in a random manner, but as distinct classes of locomotives emerged, so systems were established for numbering and for naming. The first half of the 20th century was probably the golden age of naming. Inspiration for the names was drawn from a wonderfully diverse range of sources, some predictable, some less so. Inevitably some names were used often, some infrequently: 'Falcon' has been used thirteen times, 'Redwing' only once. In the early years of British Railways the naming tradition was maintained, partly to make more acceptable the changeover from steam to diesel. More recently, naming has been a random process, usually only for short-term publicity. When locomotives die, their nameplates sometimes survive, a process that has generated a collectors' market.

▲ Military and regimental names were well used. The LNER V2 class included many locomotives but only seven were named. This plate from no. 4806 'The Green Howard' was unveiled at Richmond, Yorkshire, in 1938.

▲ For those collectors who cannot afford the real thing, there are companies that make excellent full-size replica nameplates. An example is this 'Irresistible' plate, the original of which graced an LMS Jubilee locomotive built in 1936.

▼ Nameplates are the top of the tree for railwayana collectors. This group, proudly displaying their plates, met at a private railway museum during 1986. Classic plates like these often command huge prices, often into to five figures.

▲ 'Beattie' was the name carried originally by a large tank locomotive built by the LB&SCR. In the 1930s these were rebuilt as the Remembrance class of tender locomotives. 'Beattie' ultimately became no. 32331.

▼ The LNER introduced the D49 Hunt class locomotives from 1932. 'The Morpeth', no. 62768, was built at Darlington in 1934. The nameplates carried the distinctive running fox.

▲ 'Ben Cruachan' is a typical example of a later British Railways style of nameplate, carried originally by a class 37 diesel, 37404, built in 1965. Although less valuable than steam plates, diesels are still popular.

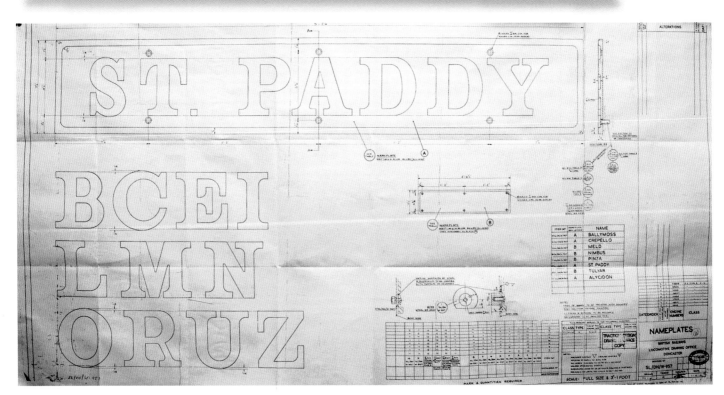

▲ Nameplates were made with great care, as this highly detailed works drawing indicates. Drawn in Doncaster in 1961, it relates to the plates for eight Deltic diesel locomotives that were to carry the names of famous racehorses: St Paddy, Ballymoss, Crepello, Meld, Nimbus, Pinza, Tulyar and Alycidon.

SCOTLAND

LOST & FOUND

RAILWAYS ADD DRAMA to the landscape, and the drama sometimes remains after they close. This is the Great Water of Fleet viaduct, in Dumfries & Galloway.

LOST & FOUND: SCOTLAND

▼ All over Britain miles of former railways have become footpaths, both official and unofficial. The former branch to Killin and Loch Tay is a splendid path through the woods, with the occasional railway telegraph pole surviving.

▶ Remarkable and unexpected things survive for decades. The Aberfeldy branch from Ballinluig, north of Perth, closed in 1965, yet in Balnaguard, a little village once served by the most minimal halt, a broken bus stop still shows the station's name.

▲ ONE OF SCOTLAND'S most remote railways was the branch to Dornoch. It closed in 1960 but there is still much to be seen, including the overgrown curve of the trackbed around Loch Fleet.

▼ MUCH OF THE KIRKCUDBRIGHT branch remains visible in the landscape, though actual exploration is not always easy. Near Tarff an old embankment crosses the fields. A large tree has grown in a gap where a little bridge used to cross a farmer's access track

BOAT OF GARTEN TO FORRES

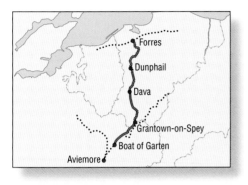

Today the main line north from Perth to Inverness sweeps north-west after Aviemore, climbing across the Monadhliadh mountains to Slochd summit and then curving down to Inverness over Culloden Moor. There is no other route, but prior to 1965 there was a choice, with another way to Inverness via Forres. Though 25 miles longer, this was originally the main line, the ambitious creation of the Inverness & Perth Junction Railway. Authorized in 1861, this line was built quickly, despite the demanding nature of the landscape. The route included high summits, dramatic viaducts, tunnels and numerous bridges, yet it opened throughout in September 1863. The engineer in charge of the line was Joseph Mitchell, and he made his mark in the quality of the decorative stonework on the viaducts and bridges. In 1865 the Inverness & Perth Junction merged with the Inverness & Aberdeen to form the Highland Railway, and it was this company that promoted and built the more direct route in use today, completing it in 1898. With this shift in emphasis, the Forres route inevitably became a secondary line, though it retained some importance through its link, via Boat of Garten, to the meandering Great North of Scotland line that ran north-eastwards through whisky country to Keith and beyond.

▲ Boat of Garten station, seen here early in the 20th century, was originally a simple stone building but was much enlarged when it became a junction. It was fully restored as part of the preserved Strathspey Railway,

◄ The Count and Countess of Seafield were supporters of the railway, and the Countess cut the first ceremonial sod to start the line's construction. At Castle Grant, their seat near Grantown, Joseph Mitchell designed this splendid castellated bridge to match the medieval-style gateway to the castle. They also had a private station.

▼ Dava summit, at 1052ft, was not the highest in Scotland but it was still a bleak place, as this photograph taken in the 1960s indicates. People walking the line today should bear this in mind.

▲ South of Dava the old line is well defined though overgrown in places. It is sometimes marked by surviving railway fencing.

This status remained largely unaltered until the 1960s when, like many secondary lines, it became a candidate for closure. This came in October 1965.

Since then, several things have helped to keep the old line alive and accessible. The section north from Aviemore to beyond Boat of Garten is now a preserved line, the Strathspey Railway, while north of Grantown-on-Spey much of the former route to Forres is a footpath, the Dava Way. It is an interesting walk, easily accessed from the A969, but bleak and remote across the high moorlands beyond Dava. Walkers must set out well prepared and well supplied. Stone bridges and a grand viaduct survive, and Dava station is now a private house. Further north, the line passes through woodlands still inhabited by red squirrels (sightings are not unusual). The path follows the track of the railway to the outskirts of Forres and then peters out among outlying estates.

▼ The viaduct that carries the trackbed 100ft above the river Divie south of Dunphail is the line's main engineering feature, and a powerful monument to its engineer, Joseph Mitchell.

ABERDEEN TO BALLATER

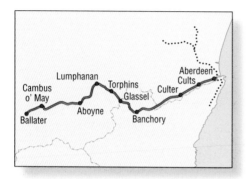

amous for its associations with Queen Victoria and Balmoral, the 43-mile-long Deeside branch to Ballater had a chequered history. The Deeside Railway was authorized to build a line from Aberdeen to Aboyne in 1846. By 1853 this was open only half way, to Banchory. Another company was then formed, the Deeside Extension Railway, to complete the line to Aboyne, which it did in 1859. Six years later yet another company, the Aboyne & Braemar, took over the baton, so to speak, and in October 1866 the railway reached Ballater. It never continued to Braemar, partly because the planned route went close to Balmoral and would have affected the royal family's privacy. Another scheme, to build a line from Ballater to Inverness, also came to nought. In the 1870s everything came under the control of the Great North of Scotland Railway. Frequent use by the royal family gave the line a certain standing and special trains ran regularly until the 1930s, carrying dispatches to Aberdeen to catch the London train. In 1904 the GNSR instituted a bus service from Ballater to Braemar.

▼ Jubilee class no. 45730, 'Ocean', waits to take its train out of Aberdeen's city centre station, the start of the journey to Ballater. The branch line swung west at Ferryhill Junction, to the north of the city, and then continued for miles along the Dee valley into an ever more remote and empty landscape.

► PERTH'S DEVELOPMENT as a major railway centre started in the 1840s. This Edwardian card hints at the complexity of lines serving the city. The main station, Perth General, is well placed for the city centre.

▼ AN ALREADY THRIVING CITY, Dundee attracted railways from the 1840s but real growth came with the opening of the first Tay bridge in 1878. This view of the Nethergate, from the North British Railway's series, was designed to encourage visitors, but on this journey there was not much time to explore.

Perth from Barnhill.

The Nethergate

North British Railway Series, Dundee

M. Wane & Co., Edinbro'. No. 1101

ARBROATH

DUNDEE

PERTH

DUNBLANE

▼ JOURNEY'S END is Catherine Street station in Arbroath, a handsome harbour town famous for its abbey, its beaches and its 'smokies'. Railways came early to Arbroath, from the late 1830s, and the converging lines from north and south gave the town three stations. Today, there is one, on the surviving line from Dundee to Aberdeen.

A SMALL SCOTCH FROM ARBROATH

HIGH STREET

ARBROATH ABBEY

ST VIGEANS CHURCH NEAR ARBROATH.

BATHING POOL & PUTTING GREEN. A.5204

EXPLORING LOST LINES

RAILWAY RAMBLERS (www.railwayramblers.org.uk)

Many have discovered the pleasures of walking old railway lines, an activity that combines an enjoyment of landscape with a sense of history and the chance of finding interesting railway structures and relics. Railway Ramblers was founded in 1978 by a group of amateur railway explorers fired by the ambition to discover and document all abandoned railways. At that time there were only about 250 miles of official railway paths in Britain and thousands of miles of closed lines, many by then in private hands. Planning walks for members was, therefore, a complex operation involving gaining permissions from many landowners, often with differing attitudes towards railway exploration. Since then the club has grown steadily; regional branches have been established, and they plan their own programmes of walks. David Shepherd OBE became president and Bill Pertwee vice-president, and the quarterly newsletter is now substantial, with numerous reports of recent explorations. The result is that all abandoned lines have been discovered and many are documented, but plenty remains to be done. Railway Ramblers has also been a significant fundraiser in this field and contributions have been made to Sustrans and other organizations to help purchase rail routes and convert them into footpaths and cycleways. Donations have also helped to preserve viaducts and other structures. Now well past its quarter century, Railway Ramblers is still pursuing its original aims, and it continues to offer to like-minded enthusiasts the chance to explore and enjoy Britain's railway past.

▼ Few closed railways still have track in place but in 1991 it could be enjoyed at Lavant, on the old line from Chichester to Midhurst, in West Sussex.

▼ Railway Ramblers take lunch on a bridge near Stichen, during a walk in 2002 along the line from Maud Junction towards Fraserburgh, Aberdeenshire.

▲ Cwm Prysor viaduct, one of the glories of the old GWR line from Blaenau Ffestiniog to Bala, in Wales, is visited by a group from the Yorkshire branch of Railway Ramblers.

SUSTRANS (www.sustrans.org.uk)

Sustrans, known originally as Sustainable Transport, was founded in Bristol in 1977 with a determination to face the problems caused by the uncontrolled growth of road traffic. The organization's primary aim was to campaign for the creation of a national network of cyclepaths all over Britain, to make it easier for people to use sustainable transport. Many paths were to be based on abandoned railway lines, and the Bristol & Bath Railway Path was the start. Since then, the National Cycle Network has grown steadily and the original target of 10,000 miles has been achieved. Today it is a huge, nationwide network of signed cycling and walking routes linking schools, stations, city centres and diverse areas of the British countryside. About one-third of the network is traffic-free. Sustrans coordinates the work of the many organizations that are creating new routes, both local and long-distance.

By raising funds on a national scale, it is able to buy or lease the necessary land, construct routes to a high standard, replace missing bridges and structures, identify the routes with seats and markers (often commissioned from artists and crafts people), and establish long-term maintenance schemes. Sustrans has incorporated hundreds of miles of former railways into its routes, greatly increasing awareness of, and access to, Britain's greatest legacy from the railway age.

▼ One of the most popular routes is the Camel Trail in Cornwall, an ideal journey along the former railway from Bodmin to Padstow.

▼ Distinctive and individual mileposts mark each Sustrans route. This example is near Cleator Moor, on a former railway in Cumbria.

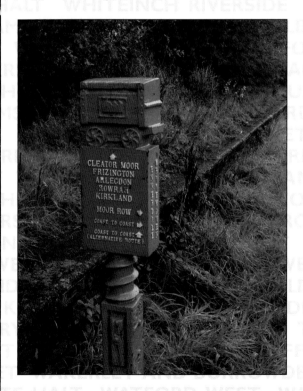

INDEX

AUTHOR'S ACKNOWLEDGEMENTS

Photographs used in this book have come from many sources. Some have been supplied by photographers or picture libraries, while others have been bought on the open market. In the latter case, photographers or libraries have been acknowledged whenever possible. However, many such images inevitably remain anonymous, despite attempts at tracing or identifying their origin. If photographs or images have been used without due credit or acknowledgement, through no fault of our own, apologies are offered. If you believe this is the case, please let us know, as we would like to give full credit in any future edition.

For special help in tracking down rare or unusual images, for being generous with items from their own collections and for help in many other ways, I am grateful to Peter Cove, David Dawes, Jane Ellis, John & Vivien Forster, Tony Harden, Dr Howard Morley, Bob Prigg, David Saunders, Andrew Swift and Nigel Willis.

Along Lost Lines is the fourth book is a series that started some years ago with *Branch Line Britain*. The processes of research, writing and production are now well established, and by and large things go quite smoothly. However, that does not in any way diminish my gratitude for the continual support, enthusiasm and expertise offered by the production team, Sue Gordon, Julian Holland and Dawn Terrey, and, last but not least, Mic Cady at David & Charles.

As ever, my greatest debt is to my wife Chrissie, whose patience and continued tolerance of all things railway after so long, and so many books, is remarkable.

PICTURE CREDITS

Unless otherwise specified, all archive photographs and ephemera are from the author's or publisher's collections.

l = left; r = right; t = top; b = bottom; m = middle

The illustrations on pages 10/11, 46/47, 86/87, 122/123, 158/159, 196/197, 232/233 are from *ABC Off By Train* (published *c*.1946–47 by Raphael Tuck & Sons Ltd).

Photographs by Paul Atterbury: title page; 6tr; 6mr; 8tl; 12/13; 14tl; 14/15b; 15tl; 15tr; 16tl; 17; 48/49; 50t; 50bl; 51; 55t; 55b; 56t; 56m; 57; 62bl; 62/63b; 63tl; 63b; 78t; 78/79b; 88/89; 90tl; 90/91; 91tr; 117tr; 118tl; 118tr; 118ml; 119ml; 119mr; 124/125; 126/127; 127tr; 132 ml; 133t; 134 tr; 134bl; 135br; 160/161; 162tl; 162/163b; 163tl; 163tr; 165b; 166/167t; 166mr; 166b; 168ml; 168b; 169tr; 170/171t; 198/199; 200t; 200br; 201; 223b; 230/231t; 231br; 234/235; 236bl; 236tr; 237t; 236/237b; 251b

Other photographs are by:

DA Anderson: 247tr
Ben Ashworth: 9br; 22ml; 43l; 71; 97t; 99tr; 115t; 133b; 215b; 222m
Associated Press: 113ml
Hugh Ballantyne: 101b; 112b; 144/145t; 188tl; 221b; 230b; 230mr; 231mr
AAF Bell: 42tr
Mark Blencowe Collection: 64/65t; 116tr
Peter F Bowles: 25b
Brighton Herald Ltd: 35
CL Caddy: 147tr

IS Carr: 231ml
HC Casserley: 64ml
Alan Cawkill: 39tr
CRL Coles: 40tr; 106/107b; 218b
Colour-Rail: 42b; 60b; 144b
K Connolly: 178ml; 179mr
CW Coslin: 82tr
Stanley Creer: 38/39t; 40/41b
Derek Cross: 43tr; 179tl; 217t; 219tl; 219b; 247tr
M Dunnett: 182ml; 221tl
Mike Esau: 59t
Kenneth Field: 37b; 72tr; 111, 119tr; 211br
JA Fleming: 113b
TG Flinders: 118b
BA Fowler: 101tr
PJ Fowler: 24/25t; 30b
John Goss: 28/29b; 43br; 83; 110b; 216b; 220tr
Tony Harden: 18tr; 23tr; 26ml; 26br; 54ml; 56b; 67tl; 67ml; 68/69t; 68/69b; 75ml; 75r; 75tr; 92/93b; 93t; 94tr; 95tr; 95m; 98tr; 102mr; 102bl; 129tl; 130tr; 132b; 134/135b; 135t; 138ml; 139mr; 141bl; 150bl; 150t; 150mr; 151tr; 151mr; 151bl; 152t; 152mr; 153tr; 153b; 164tl; 165tl; 165m; 167b; 169b; 172/173t; 172mr; 172b; 173tr; 173mr; 173b; 174tl; 175tr; 184tr; 184t; 184mr; 184bl; 205b; 212bl; 213ml; 227br; 229tl; 238ml; 242b; 243t; 244b; 248/249b; 249tr; 249m
CS Heaps: 16b
GF Heiron: 34t
GT Heavyside: 146b
Julian Holland: 21t; 21b; 22tr; 21/22b; 58/59b; 72b; 94b; 95b; 96/97b; 98/99b; 128/129b; 130/131b; 131tl; 136b; 203ml; 203tl; 204tr; 204b; 205t; 207b; 208/209t; 209b; 222b; 223tr; 238b; 239t; 240/241; 243br; 244/245t;

245b; 251tr
Robert Humm & Co: 85tr
Derek Huntriss: 53b; 105tl
Alan Jarvis: 61t; 73b; 114b; 116br; 118mr; 135m; 142/143b
DK Jones: 73t
MA King: 85b
Locomotive & General: 25t; 31b; 148b
Michael Mensing: 24bl; 70bl; 70tr; 105b; 179bl; 208b; 216tr; 220b
Howard S Morley: 210/211b
SJ Morley: 210bl
Gavin Morrison: 52ml; 115b; 210/211t
Newcastle Chronicle & Journal: 111tr, 112 (insets)
Peter Oliver (David Spaven collection): 239b
R Payne: 142/143t
Ivo Peters Collection: 68bl; 69br
C Plant: 218tr
DMH Platt: 148tr; 149tr; 149ml
Railway Ramblers: 250tr; 250bl; 250br
GA Richardson
Gerald T Robinson 116bl
E H Sawford: 147b; 214tr
Sealink (BRB): 227tl
WS Sellar: 106tl
Brian Sharpe: 40bl
Frank Spaven (David Spaven collection): 77m; 141tl
AE Staples: 180tr
Brian Stephenson: 246b
J Stockwell: 202b; 203tr; 203b
Sussex Express & County Herald: 64b
Andrew Swift: 65mr; 76mr; 128ml; 184bl; 185tr
Douglas Thompson: 137b
Mike Turner: 144ml
Graham Wise: 20bl; 192tr